Working Psychoanalytically with Infants

Working Psychoanalytically with Infants: From Françoise Dolto to Zhuang Zhou explores several case studies from Nicole Yvert Coursilly's work in French care homes, providing psychoanalytic treatment to babies who had suffered traumatic experiences.

The book describes the clinical sessions in detail, as well as their surprisingly rapid beneficial effects. Coursilly explores the importance of body-language when working with pre-verbal children and shows how work with infants can help bolster an analyst's skill when working with older children and adolescents. The case studies include work with babies under the age of 1, as well as toddlers. The author introduces the work of philosophers and analysts throughout, to illustrate her ideas.

This enlightening book will be of interest to all practicing and training psychoanalysts, as well as child psychotherapists, psychiatrists and care workers.

Nicole Yvert Coursilly is a psychoanalyst in private practice based in Paris, France. She has worked as a clinician in the public sector and in non-profit organisations for thirty years, and as a psychoanalytic psychotherapist in psychiatric hospitals for both children and adults. She is former president of *Espace-Enfance*, an association for the training of personnel specialised in early childhood.

"Nicole Yvert detects the potential vitality present in the most helpless children, who have already faced unspeakable disaster. She trusts that each of them harbours a desire for an other, and she prepares the way for the life force to resume its course in them by passing through her. Indeed, the entire burgeoning psychic activity of an infant, expressed in his body, tends towards an other, it seeks the psychic life and the words of another speaking being.

But it is not only the words which heal; beyond the words, there is the vibrant energy animating the body of the living, speaking person. Nicole Yvert identifies the signs through which the body can speak – a sort of sign language (the little human emits signals in search of someone who can receive them) – or a sort of graphic language. The analyst offers her listening, listening which deciphers: her action as a witness-sign reader transforms these signs into an existential statement which ties both her and the infant to humanity through the common bond of speech."

> **Pascale Hassoun,** *psychoanalyst and clinical psychologist, founding member of Cercle Freudien and its former president. Founder of Che Vuoi journal. Between 2003 and 2016, contributed to the creation of the Chengdu Psychoanalytic Center (China).*

"In the scarcely hundred pages of her book, Nicole Yvert tells the story of a non-negotiable minimum: that sought by an infant in his relation to the helpful other – here, the analyst – the minimum needed by his vitality to take hold of the thread of a life uniquely his. Providing this minimum is quite demanding. Access to the tools of psychoanalytic theory does not exempt the analyst from 'thinking his place' and from redefining it day after day. The author describes herself humbly as a 'clairvoyant witness', a 'tuner' of human instruments, a catalyst, interacting with a singular other who is not to be reduced to his catastrophic entrance into the world. The work takes place at a more fundamental level: the level of life energy which connects the infant with the other who responds to his quest. Who gives to whom?

Based on her long experience, Nicole Yvert asserts that both protagonists gain stronger bonds with their humanity."

> **Philippe Jousset,** *literature professor, Université Aix-Marseille, Marseille, France.*

"In *Working Psychoanalytically with Infants*, Nicole Yvert leads the reader to the scene of her work as an analyst with pre-verbal patients. She describes simply, clearly and with great sensitivity her manner of entering into transference with these children who, having been removed from their families and entrusted to an infant care home or a foster home, are waiting to hear a true account of these events – the truth that can reawaken their desire to live.

We are in awe of her dazzling interpretations, even as she explains how she can decipher on a baby's body the trauma that no one before her has been able to put into words for him.

She presents the elements constituting the support she needs to play this singular and trying role in the lives of these babies. She draws support from two sources: the theory developed by Freud and his disciples, and Chinese thought on the void, this companion of availability uniquely suited to the perceptions of signs. Reading this book leaves the reader unsettled, perhaps even transformed. It constitutes an exceptional experience for a reader receptive to the vitality to which it testifies."

José Morel Cinq-Mars, *psychoanalyst and author.*

Working Psychoanalytically with Infants

From Françoise Dolto to Zhuang Zhou

Nicole Yvert Coursilly

Translated by Agnès Jacob

Routledge
Taylor & Francis Group

LONDON AND NEW YORK

Designed cover image: © SHU-LING LIN

First published in English 2026
by Routledge
4 Park Square, Milton Park, Abingdon, Oxon OX14 4RN

and by Routledge
605 Third Avenue, New York, NY 10158

Routledge is an imprint of the Taylor & Francis Group, an informa business

Translated by Agnès Jacob

Published in French by Editions des crépuscules 2017

British Library Cataloguing-in-Publication Data
A catalogue record for this book is available from the British Library

ISBN: 978-1-041-11762-9 (hbk)
ISBN: 978-1-041-11716-2 (pbk)
ISBN: 978-1-003-67279-1 (ebk)

DOI: 10.4324/9781003672791

Typeset in Times New Roman
by Newgen Publishing UK

To all the little ones with whom I shared exceptional moments,

to Juliette,

to Clara.

Contents

Acknowledgements   *x*
Rationale   *xi*

1 Context: Stories: Individual and Collective   1

2 Clinical Work: Narratives and Scenes   19

3 Language, Words and The Body   76

4 Transference with Little Humans   86

5 On Availability and Transference   94

Closing   110

Bibliography   *118*
Index   *121*

Acknowledgements

My warmest thanks go to the infant home workers and Child Welfare Services workers who entrusted the children to my care and accompanied them. Without their devotion, their active participation, their confidence in me and in psychoanalysis, none of this would have been possible. This essay is the culmination of a collective endeavour in which everyone had a part to play.

I would like to express my gratitude to Anne Champion for her boundless generosity. The finesse of her tactful editing, as well as her well-founded and well-advised comments at every stage of the writing made the publication of this book possible.

I am grateful to the colleagues with whom I worked in reflection groups. Their loyal presence, their listening and our exchanges have nourished my reflection over the years.

I wish to thank Emmanuelle Touati, whose generous professional talents proved invaluable.

My thanks also go to Pierre Champion, a rigorous and tireless proofreader.

I thank Caroline Éliacheff, whose confidence in me launched this clinical adventure.

Last but not least, I would like to thank François Jullien for having exposed me to new conceptual possibilities.

Rationale

"May the child's voice in him never be silenced, may it fall like a gift from the sky offering to dried-out words the brilliance of his laughter, the salt of his tears, his all-powerful savagery."

Louis-René Des Forêts, *Ostinato*.[1]

After working as a psychologist, then as a psychoanalyst, in various structures – public, semi-public, private – I now look back on fifty years of professional activity. Can I identify a life-sustaining thread, can I discern and offer a reliable, solid element to help us move forward in this changing contemporary world in relentless turmoil?

My concern is of a double nature. The first, on a practical level, is rooted in political and social reality: to continue and strengthen our efforts in the sphere of mental health, disease prevention and treatment in public institutions; to transmit and update our inheritance in the field of psychoanalysis of very young children. The second, on a theoretical level, concerns the usefulness of analytic listening. I shall try to give a description of it, showing its evolution as a concept and practice. I will give an indication of how it is acquired and preserved. What we will look at are not the mechanisms and laws of human psychic functioning, or the subject's relation to the object, based on a solipsistic model. Rather, we will consider the strategic

conditions creating effectivity in the transference, the foremost
concern of the psychoanalyst in his practice, because it brings
about in the *in-between*[2] two subjects, two living beings, two
existences, the one and the other.

Psychoanalytic theories[3] are mainly concerned with the
development and function of what Freud called the psychic
apparatus. These elements form the focus of the practitioner's
training, and they accompany him is his ensuing work. They
are his support, they constitute his points of reference. Thanks
to them, he is not alone in his solitary practice. In addition, they
serve as bridges to the collective domain, allowing the analyst
to speak to other individuals and to other disciplines. However,
they cannot replace his own thinking. The work carried out in
analysis must pass through his person, his body and his thinking
process. How does the teaching of his masters express itself in
him? How is he influenced? How does the analyst enable spontaneous speech – which will prove effective – to flow freely
between him and his patient?

My psychoanalytic experience with traumatised babies,
infants separated from their families in dramatic circumstances,
provided me with material gleaned from intimate knowledge,
allowing me to try to answer these essential questions.

The change of viewpoint brought about by my encounter
with Chinese philosophy and the Chinese language, through the
works of eminent specialists, gave me access to a new modality
for elucidating this experience, for shedding light on the effectivity of the analytic situation. This is what the present essay will
attempt to describe.

Notes

1 Des Forêts, L.-R., *Ostinato*, Cows, M.A. (Trans.), University of
  Nebraska Press, 2002.
2 Here, *in-between* is used as a noun, referring to the term elucidated
  by François Jullien in his first lecture as holder of the Chair of

Otherness, on December 8, 2011, and published by Galilée under the title *L'écart et l'entre.*

3 The plural refers to the theoretical works of authors who, in Freud's era and subsequently, have contributed to the psychoanalytic corpus founded by Freud.

Chapter 1

Context

Stories: Individual and Collective

Overview

Freud's genius consisted, first of all, in bringing to light a psychic sphere previously unexplored, which he named the unconscious... the active depths always at work that each of us probes and endows with meaning in his own way. These depths have been recognised since ancient times, but were not regarded as a distinct agency separate from consciousness. Today neuroscience has rendered its activity visible in images. We have learned that 90% of our neuronal activity is unconscious; what is conscious is only 10% of this activity.

Freud created the concept of *the unconscious* and described it in the language of the Western world of the late 19th century and the early 20th century, an era which saw the explosion of knowledge in science and the rapid development of industry. He conceived and outlined a model of the psychic apparatus and a medicine of the soul which also treats the body; hysteria is located at his intersection. Freud inscribed this medicine in the domain of the applied sciences, where science and philosophy intersect. Thus, from its beginnings, psychoanalysis has been inseparable from its application, that is, from its verifiable effects.

Today, wherever psychic care is being dispensed, psychoanalysis is on trial, asked to justify itself. The tempestuous debates that followed the publication of the decision of the French National Authority for Health,[1] stating that because of

DOI: 10.4324/9781003672791-1

"lack of consensus on its effectiveness" psychoanalysis is "not recommended" in the treatment of autistic children, revealed not only the deep resentment created by practices which had placed a burden of guilt on families, but also the violent power struggle and the financial stakes involved.

Since then, a different trend, coming from the American continent, has become predominant. Now, what matters are evaluation scales and classification. The symptom must be detected and eradicated; its meaning and value are ignored. The DSM[2] reigns supreme. Psychoanalysis has been ousted from the universities, and discredited in the sphere of madness. It is given very little place in psychiatry, suffering the same fate as institutional psychotherapy, which has been the pillar of French psychiatry in the past 50 years. And who still remembers psychopathology? From now on, we speak of "handicap". We re-educate, we rehabilitate, we adapt. Child psychiatrists/psychotherapists are rare; physicians are no longer trained to exercise this function as heads of institutions or departments. Without such specialists, these places of treatment will disappear or be relocated, despite huge demand for intervention and ever-longer waiting lists.

We must admit that in its golden age, in the seventies, psychoanalysis acted unwisely: it lacked modesty; in its arrogance, it declared itself all-powerful, capable of theorising everything, treating everything. Its word was gospel, the truth about "the human" divested of its problems. Now, this arrogance has come back to haunt it.

Yet, what do we actually see happening?

Psychoanalysis entered the general hospital to treat the body in tandem with medicine, in oncology, in neonatal care, in paediatrics and in intensive care. It is present in Social Services, particularly in emergency housing, group homes, child-parent therapy programs, nurseries. It is employed in the analysis of various services. In the mental health field, it participates in multiple-treatment programs – for instance, as an aspect of the

treatment offered to autistic children[3] – where different disciplines work together, rather than competing. In the community,
it guides the reflection of those who run child-parent care facilities, founded by educator Hélène Malandrin and Françoise
Dolto, and called "*La Maison verte*" (Green House). Their aim
was to "bring psychoanalysis into the community", as Dolto
said, as part of a civic project in support of individuals and for
educational purposes. Today, *maisons vertes* are springing up
everywhere in France and throughout the world.

Our hope is that psychoanalysis ceases to be fascinating, to
inspire either passion or loathing; that its message ceases to be
heard as prophetic, but becomes a message among others and in
dialogue with them, that it be a tool in the service of thinking,
of life, of man and of society.

And what do we see in artistic and literary milieux? In 2013,
the Prix Médicis was awarded to Marie Darrieussecq, writer
and psychoanalyst, for *Il faut beaucoup aimer les hommes*. The
same year, the Goncourt Prize was awarded to psychologist
and author Pierre Lemaitre, for *Au revoir là-haut* (The Great
Swindle); and, in 2014, the same prize went to Lydie Salvayre,
psychiatrist-psychoanalyst, for *Pas pleurer*. These novels tell
personal stories, unique accounts of suffering, love, alliances,
passions, births… against the background of History with its
cycles of barbaric destruction and enthusiastic reconstruction,
its class struggles and its fights for freedom. Just like in the
psychoanalyst's sphere of work.

In France, we had Raymond Dorgelès, Henri Barbusse, Louis-
Ferdinand Céline, Charles Péguy and many others to testify to
their wars. Three or four generations later, now that psychoanalysis is available to us, writers have often put history into
words through the intermediary of another person, a living witness who enables them to breathe life into the narrative. In the
meantime, Jorge Semprun, Primo Levi and others have testified
to frozen memory, immobilised in the icy sea of trauma – "snow
in the memory", as François Maspero[4] says about the vagueness

surrounding his father's death in Mauthausen, to which Semprun referred in his book *The Long Voyage*.[5] All of these poignant books carry out work on memory. In his investigations, Patrick Modiano, recent Nobel Prize winner, tries to melt this "snow in the memory", in order to uncover traces of vanished lives, traces that evaporated. Like in the lives of our patients.

The same is true for the fields of cinema, television, theatre, dance, music, architecture – in short, all the arts, whose content and form have been influenced by a psychoanalytic perspective. In the writing of fragments, discontinuity, flashes of inspiration and memory breakthroughs construct a different kind of narrative.

In France and elsewhere, psychoanalysis has sown its seeds in the culture, and is disseminated by cultural productions. As a result, it is continually transmitted from the individual to the collective. This psychoanalysis is more concerned with trauma than with the sexual, the sexual being the element which, from the depths of trauma, brings us back to the singularity of a life. The task of psychoanalysis is to assist the emergence of life, everywhere.

The artist is the one entrusted with this task, as Élie Faure expressed it, speaking of Rembrandt:

> Because Rembrandt is the only one who was always present in everything that he looked at, he is the only one who dared to mix mud with the light of the eyes, to introduce fire into ashes, to cause a pink or a pale blue, as fresh as a flower, to glow in a shroud. When he comes, all moral categories disappear, to let the triumphant torrent of life, ever reborn, pour through the night, spurt forth from sepulchers, and cover putrescence and death with phosphorescent shadows in which new germs unfold.[6]

The cultural world is nourished by psychoanalysis because many creative people – writers, actors, directors, producers, painters, musicians, professors and critics – have encountered it personally, as patients. Does our dehumanising society, so barbaric, so cruel and so destructive of life, produce the urgent need to seek another, one who is present – the psychoanalyst, for instance – to reconnect with the spark of life?

Once Change Intervenes, What Remains the Same?

The Virtue of Listening

Theories are the expression of each author's thought development: each one writes the score for his instrument and takes up the motif to play in the great concert of ideas, brilliantly, with virtuosity, diligently, step by step. But these theories have often tended to become dogmas, at least for a while. It is then up to clinical practice to ensure that they are constantly brought into question. This questioning evolves, of course, with geopolitical and socio-political changes, but the cornerstone on which it is founded is the humanising effect of analytic listening.

Its virtues have been known since ancient times, as revealed in texts dating back to the origins of Christianity, as well as in Chinese texts. I would like to shed light on this question using the tools pertaining to my work, in order to arrive at what is essential, the minimally necessary principles.

I gathered these thinking tools from my life experiences, from my encounters, in my working world, in the health care institutions where I was employed, in psychoanalytic institutions to which I belonged; as well as from the art world: painting, literature; and from the world of ideas where I encountered Chinese philosophy. I was always introduced into these worlds by guides, but the aim was always to come to understand them on my own.

Charting a Life Course in Psychoanalysis: a Trajectory

My work in psychoanalysis developed along two axes. The work with adults consisted of consultations, psychotherapy and psychoanalytic treatment. Many of these adults were not coming "for analysis", as they were prompt to tell me. They came because they were suffering, needed to talk to someone, to hear what someone else had to say, because they had no words to say and to think through what was unsaid in their lives, in the submerged portion of their existence which was pulling them into darkness. They had been sent to me in hopes of rectifying this. They did not want to be met with silence, and almost always expressed this wish directly. They had heard from friends or in the media about analyses where the analyst remained silent for years, or they had experienced this themselves with a previous analyst. They came to encounter the other in themselves, and in the one sitting across from them, so that finally "someone" would talk to them, answer them. So that they would no longer be alone and speechless. They came to delve into their own depths and, at the same time, offer another person access to this inner realm.

> Let us start from the level of language itself. [...] The intimate is what lies at the deepest place in the being. We speak of "intimate conviction", and of the "intimate structure of things", meaning their essential composition. The intimate is also that which creates close ties at the deepest level; we say: "intimate connection", "intimate relations", to "be in intimate terms with..." In all its meanings, the "intimate" brings about a reversal: that which is most interior and which consequently implies its own limitation, also disposes towards openness to the other.[7]

The second axis was my work with children, and particularly with babies. With them, the demand for an interlocutor who must hear and speak the words needed to give them access to their lives – to the other of the encounter – is even more evident, immediate and direct. The mystery of effective speech was most profound in my work with infants, seen without their parents, since they had been separated from them and entrusted to Social Services. After I left institutions, institutions came to me: babies, whom I had previously seen in PPMCs (Psycho-Pedagogical Medical Centres) came to my office accompanied by their child care assistants. The consultations were paid for by the departments where the Centres were located. But what made the consultations possible was the combined work of psychologists in the institutions, and Child Welfare Services inspectors.

Still, how can we speak of psychoanalysis with babies when babies don't have speech? Who speaks, when they don't even have their parents to speak for them? The analyst? It makes sense to ask these questions, but the paradox is merely illusory. Let's not forget that language includes the nonverbal and that children can have spokespersons other than their parents. In any case, following in the footsteps of Françoise Dolto, I set out on this path. At the Paul-Manchon d'Antony orphanage, with the team providing patient care, Dolto developed a clinical work protocol which included psychoanalysis and involved all the personnel. In 1988, when I started to see babies placed in this orphanage, Françoise Dolto had just died. Over the past 20 years, she had encouraged a process of transmission among those who worked with her.

Dolto was accused of practicing magic by talking to babies. Those of us who worked with children in analysis felt we had to defend ourselves against this somewhat scornful accusation, an accusation of recourse to unscientific practices. In truth, we should have been proud of working this magic! In our Western societies with their scientific ideal, we think we can ignore the mystery of the effects of speech. When I say "magic", I mean the magic we depict to our children: "Once there was a magician...". Is this not a way of confirming the vital power of words and formulas spoken in a certain situation, where their action brings about a transformation?

Recently, at a concert, I had the good fortune of being seated at the back of the stage, that is, facing the conductor and very close to him. This allowed me to see, feel and experience a marvellous phenomenon: Andris Nelsons was playing the music like an actor playing a part, he played the musical score literally, he was played by the score, he was music. He was embodying the music in his own body and that of the orchestra. It was amazing! Sviatoslav Richter used to say that the musical movement should flow into the body. This is how babies play their score: their bodies play and the script flows into their bodies. Lisbeth Gruwez, a Flemish dancer, expresses her experience of this by saying that it is as if she dances to a script written internally. Indeed, when I saw her dance, the vision that offered itself to me was that of a body writing a text, a living calligraphy.

We think with music, we think with the paintbrush, we think with the body. In the intervals between painting, music and dance, we must find words. In *Journey to the End of the Night*, Céline says:

> Not much music left inside us to dance to. Our youth has gone to the ends of the earth to die in the silence of the truth. And where, I ask you, can a man escape to […]? The truth is death.[8]

The analyst must discover (rediscover) the music of life, endow the script with sound and an interpretation, set life dancing… all the more because death is at work. No, the truth of this world is not death, but life-death. Life and death are inseparable, as Chinese philosophy – a philosophy of process and transformation – teaches us. The same teaching was imparted by Heraclitus, a pre-Socratic Greek philosopher of the 5th and 4th centuries B.C.:

> Everything is in constant flux and opposite things are identical, so that the same thing is good and bad at the same time […] The same thing in us is living and dead; both living and dying are in all living and in all dying.[9]

This experience, this clinical practice – psychoanalysis with babies in institutions – is the work I chose, to try to solve the mystery of the effects of speech, at its roots. Countless interconnected memories resurfaced. Scenes emerged from the depths of my memory, prompted by the need to write. I realised they were memories of moments in my life, moments that had changed me. They had brought me pain, joy, anguish, strength. They had expanded my range of emotions, improved my representational capacity. They had allowed me to piece together my history, to reintegrate my "cut-out impressions", to use Françoise Davoine's term.[10]

These moments had endowed me with the ability to reflect on the fact of having been born in 1945, on July 25 – the day when Harry Truman, the President of the United States, authorised the use of "Little Boy" to bomb Hiroshima – the fact of being a child of the war, as Patrick Modiano described himself in his Nobel Prize acceptance speech in 2014 in Stockholm. Not only did my birth coincide with my grandfather's death – personal history – but also with the threat of annihilation of entire populations – world history, reawakening echoes of the first catastrophe, the Great War. My parents, our parents, had been through two world wars, between 1914 and 1918 when they were children, and between 1939 and 1945, in their youth. I and those of my generation grew up amid the rubble of trauma and destruction, in the shadow of familial melancholias, in a time of reconstruction of ruins. The soil in which we took root was composed of the earth of the cemeteries and mass graves of the 20th century.

In other words, when one comes into the world surrounded by the stench of death, what hope, what inspiration, what existence is possible? And we know that today the catastrophes are everywhere, all the time; personal and collective catastrophes, visible or invisible… The stakes are high. These were the circumstances in which the babies I saw were born between 1985 and 2015; it was a situation I myself was confronting when I encountered them.

The stories of these children resonated at the deepest level with my personal history, with History and with the history of child psychoanalysis, which had its start during the Second World War. Melanie Klein and Anna Freud, who had been in conflict since the 1930s about the definition of the "educational" – among other things – were the two major theoreticians in this field at the time. Their disagreement became particularly marked during and after the war, especially after Anna opened a shelter for child survivors of concentration camps. Were her aims observational or were they therapeutic?

Donald Winnicott, who had been Klein's analysand, was seeing children during the London bombings; at the same period, Françoise Dolto was working in paediatrics at a Paris hospital. She had been a student of Sophie Morgenstern, the first analyst in France to conduct psychoanalysis with children, and to introduce the use of drawing in child psychotherapy. As Dolto became known for her remarkable work at the hospital, other practitioners started to send her children whose symptoms resisted treatment. Such symptoms included enuresis, with which a whole population of little boys was suddenly afflicted after the war. Dolto thought that they suffered from narcissistic devaluation in their phallic identification with their fathers who, they were told, had been "made prisoners". If they were imprisoned, they must have done something bad, which meant that their sons could no longer be proud of them. In response, these children regressed to an earlier "unconscious body image", as her theory described. Thus, Dolto was establishing a connection between emotions, psychic conflicts and somatic manifestations. In fact, the title of her doctoral thesis had been: *Psychoanalysis and Paediatrics.* Not surprisingly, one of Winnicott's books is entitled: *Through Paediatrics to Psychoanalysis*.

The catastrophes that befell Europe – bombings, roundups, fathers taken to forced labour camps, parents and families sent to death camps – resulted in children being abandoned, orphaned, in hiding, separated. It was in this context that child psychoanalysis developed – in this extreme situation where rendering assistance was a matter of life or death, just as it often is today. Child psychotherapy developed in hospitals, nurseries and other types of residences for children, where what René Spitz identified in 1945 as "hospitalism" was observed. In these institutions, it was noted that "miracles" occurred when the staff engaged in verbal interactions with the children. Various archive documents – therapy accounts, films – attest to this. In these places, it was clear from the beginning that verbal exchanges were vitally important for babies, for the development of the body, as well as the psyche. It was clear that for a baby, having a psychic connection with someone is an absolute priority. We owe the foundational work in this field to Rosine Lefort, Jenny Aubry, Serge Lebovici and Michel Soulé.

We can imagine the importance of the concept of "trauma" in the analytic research and practice of this period. Ferenczi's trauma concept, developed and discussed throughout his work, concerns early harm, harm inflicted before language acquisition to the child's environment; the development of his concept also includes the serious repercussions of such harm on the psychic construction of the child. These early injuries can be caused by History, such as the wars we mentioned. Or they can originate in the mother's and the family's psychic reality (hallucinations, delusions, depression), which bring about discordant, inadequate responses to the child's demands. The madness of History creates private madness.

Prerequisite for Discussing Child Psychoanalysis: Relation Between Treatment, Education, Psychotherapy-Psychoanalysis

Psychoanalysts who have conducted analysis with children, who have taught the subject and written about it, know that the therapeutic, educational and psychological dimensions arc closely tied. They are not to be blended together, but rather seen as going hand in hand, each one separate, but opposite each other. They are different, close but different; the border between them is porous, but it exists.

My teachers were Françoise Dolto, my contemporary, and Donald Winnicott, through the reading of his texts. Both had been paediatricians before becoming analysts, and both gave preference to conversation as a mode of transmission. Everyone has heard of Dolto's phone-in radio show called *Lorsque l'enfant paraît* (When the Baby Shows Up), which was met with sharp criticism from psychoanalysts but had a great impact on the audience. This was part of her commitment to bring "psychoanalysis into the life of the city", which she then pursued by creating the "Green Houses" with Marie-Hélène Malandrin; the success of these meeting places for parents and children has never diminished, in France or anywhere else in the world. Winnicott's collection of essays, *Talking to Parents*, is perhaps less well known. Both of them left us numerous transcripts of conference talks, as well as works with a theoretical focus, all of them innovative, inventive and freedom-enhancing.

Later, I discovered that my ideas were in agreement with those of another Anglo-Saxon author, Wilfred Bion, who had spent his childhood in India, exposed to a philosophy of transition, transformation, non-separation; and to the "not without the other" attitude of a subject always perceived in context. Anglo-Saxons have historical ties with Asia through the Indies.

For psychoanalysts who have worked with children, combining the therapeutic with the educational and the psychological makes perfect sense. The child, who is in a process of becoming, comes to see the analyst when he is assailed by neurosis, by the madness of his family environment, or by internal or external events (such as a handicap or an illness), because he cannot escape this assault on his own. He calls for help and his distress calls are considerably strident. He is looking for a witness.

Through transference, the psychoanalyst intervenes not only to untie the knots in the history, in the child's psychic construction, but also to tie together, to weave, to help with this construction and enable the child to find his own path and set off on the course of his life.[11] The psychoanalyst puts pain into words: the child's pain, the family's pain, the ancestors' pain, that of those involved with the child, in order to render it thinkable, communicable, to dissolve shame and thereby repair the social link which has been attacked, erased, made impossible. This intervention also serves to handle limits and frustrations, inscribing them in the analytic frame. The analyst addresses the child, his family or his caregivers, depending on the situation.

His job is not to tell the parents how to bring up the child. But he can give them advice when he becomes aware, in the transference, that they have lacked advice and that they would welcome it and put it to good use. He will support them in their educational role as rule-makers, and in their consent to forgo being always loved. The analyst will also voice the suffering they endured as a result of being left alone, without support or understanding – putting an end to their solitude by doing so. The psychoanalyst can express his approval or disapproval, remind the child of certain rules of socialisation, but he remains aware that he is his parents' child and that this is what will determine his psychic development. Parents must always be considered worthy, no matter how they act, simply because they are part of the human species, Françoise Dolto liked to say, and I agree with her.

The educational and therapeutic aspect of the analyst's role is inherent to the protocol of the session, to its rhythm: beginning and end of sessions, separation and coming together again, delimited time and space; the analyst's manner of treating the child, the fact that he imposes limits which must be respected absolutely (otherwise he puts an end to the session); this contributes to the child's psychic development and capacity for social interaction. The analyst never forgets that the child is the subject of an ongoing process, a process of psychic construction. All this is part of what I inherited from Françoise Dolto, made my own and brought to life – a legacy that always proved profitable. Her views differed from those of other child psychoanalysts like Edmond and Marie-Cécile Ortigues, who insisted that there can be no child analysis without both parents present. Dolto had a larger view. Her practice was founded on the principle that listening to a child presupposes the respect of his double filiation. Primary narcissism, the bedrock of psychic construction, depends on it. Fortunately, this made it conceivable to treat children in the absence of their parents, who might be dead, vanished, hospitalised, imprisoned... This view was the foundation of my practice.

Agnès Dupont-Link recounted this interchange that took place regularly in a child's therapy, at the beginning of the session: "Show me my father", M. asks, and we look together through his file for the paragraph where it is written: "Name of father: unknown".[12] In this context, I will quote a passage from Ivan Jablonka's book *A History of the Grandparents I Never Had*:

Archives of the City of Paris [...] The prison records confirm that M. J. [the grandfather who disappeared in the camps, a man the author's father had barely known and whose trace the author is seeking to discover, as proof of his existence] was incarcerated [and] transferred to the Fresnes prison [for being an undocumented foreigner without residency papers on French territory, although he had been officially ordered to leave the country]. [...] the register of the 16th chamber of criminal courts for the Seine region. We page through the volume feverishly, our emotion at a peak: there he is.

I believe that I became a historian so that one day, I could make that discovery. The distinction we make between our family stories [...] and what we like to call History with its pompous capital H, makes little sense. They are in every way the same. [...] To do history is to lend an ear to the pulse of the silence, to attempt to replace an anguish [...] with the sweet sorrowful respect the human condition inspires in us. [...]. And when I run my hand over these court registers, allowing my eyes to follow the flow of the clerk's cursive script, I feel an indescribable sense of relief.[13]

The word *father* – unknown, therefore existing – written in the psychoanalyst's file, as well as the name of the grandfather written in an official register, certify, legitimate, make official the existence of this relative, and the subject's feeling of being alive.

The position of the analyst in his work with children must conform to a code of ethics governing the conduct of all social workers and other professionals involved in educating other people's children; this code of ethics includes an attitude of respect towards their parents, regardless of the latter's conduct. This does not mean siding with the parents when they mistreat the child or behave badly, but they must be treated with the respect due to all human beings, and without judgment. Judgment must be left to the justice system. This is even more vital when the analyst sees children placed in public institutions, brought to them not by their parents, but by third parties. And even more so when the patients are babies: with them this rule acquires its full significance and fully demonstrates its usefulness.

The psychoanalyst is not required to teach or to provide physical care, but he must make sure that someone does this, because he cannot start therapy with a child whose needs have not been met. If need be, he must intercede on the child's behalf. Analytic work can only begin once basic care has been provided.

This lengthy preamble is important because there are preconditions to verbal therapy. There are different levels of listening: if a child appears to be undernourished, he must be fed before suffering from hunger is verbalised by the analyst. If a child is abused, the mistreatment must be brought to an end; if he is subjected to incest, this situation must be resolved in reality. The child's analyst is first and foremost a responsible adult and law-abiding citizen, required to offer assistance. Therapy cannot be conducted in a perverse situation recognised as such; doing so would constitute complicity. Thus, psycho-therapy cannot be practiced in the absence of education and adequate care. The psychotherapist's work is built on that of educators and caregivers.

A Method: to See Clearly

The mystery of what is experienced along these journeys called "cures", or simply during consultations, these apparently magical transformations that take place, prompted me to inves-tigate this process more closely.

I will illustrate my method with a quote from Zhuang Zhou, a Chinese thinker from the third century BC, translated into French by Jean-François Billeter, in *Études sur Tchouang-tseu*: "Rather than defending a perspective the other rejects and rejecting the perspective he defends, it is better to clarify",[14] literally "to make use of clarity". Making a daring parallel, Billeter quotes from Wittgenstein's *On Certainty*:

The difficulty [...] is not that of finding the solution [...]. [We are] wrongly expecting a solution, whereas the solution of the difficulty is a description, if we give it the right place in our considerations. If we dwell upon it, and do not try to get beyond it. The difficulty here is: to stop.[15]

To stop – that is what we do for the duration of a session; it is what I try to do while I write.

In his book *Take a Closer Look*, Daniel Arasse initiates us to the playful practice of a mode of thinking allowing us to perceive what we do not see in a painting, the invisible, the painter's conceptual thinking, "the object of an imperceptible intuition, something that can be thought but not experienced",[16] he tells us, the deciphering of the thought of the painter who thinks with his brushes. This is accomplished through description. "To make use of clarity": thus, description will be one of my tools.

When I decided to retire, to close my office, I found myself wanting to testify to the transformations I helped to bring about, to talk about them with others who had witnessed them as I had. To tell the stories of these children, to listen to different accounts, to look at these events closely and describe them – in other words, to represent the scenes faithfully.

These scenes emerge radiant and clear now, in the writing, but when they unfolded I was in shock as I discovered the power of my speech, of my presence; I was amazed by the surging forth of life in which I participated, most often not knowing how, simply engaging in a process, with occasional flashes of brilliance.

It may be that I became a psychoanalyst to experience these moments.

Notes

1 The decision was not preceded by any debate, and resulted in a return to the behaviourism of the start of the 20th century, ignoring subsequent neuroscientific and cognitive research which condemns behaviourist reductionism and confirms many of the intuitions formulated by psychoanalysts. See Crespin, G.C., *Traitement des troubles du spectre autistique*, érès, 2013, Preface by J. Hochmann.

2 The first *Diagnostic and Statistical Manual of Mental Disorders* was published in 1952 by the team of Robert Spitzer. Today's latest version is the DSM-V.

3 See the work of the UDAC: *Unité d'accompagnement* PRÉAUT. See also Crespin, G.C., *Traitement des troubles du spectre autistique*, érès, 2013, and the work of Pierre Delion.

4 Maspero, F., *Les abeilles et la guêpe*, Seuil, 2002.

5 Semprun, J., *The Long Voyage*, Seaver, R. (Trans.), New York: The Overlook Press, 2005.

6 Faure, E., *History of Art* III, Pack, W. (Trans.), New York and London: Harper & Brothers, 1924.

7 Jullien, F., *De l'intime, loin du bruyant amour*, Grasset, 2013; quoted loosely from p. 23 and p. 26.

8 Céline, L.-F., *Journey to the End of the Night*, New York: New Directions, 2006.

9 Heraclitus, *Fragments*, Penguin Classics, 2003.

10 Davoine, F., *Wittgenstein's Folly*, Routledge, 2023. "I call cut-out impressions those inscriptions of events which have not been repressed."

11 To quote Jean-Max Gaudillière, speaking at the 2014 *Psyche and Cancer* Conference: "When faced with distress, I weave". See also Golder, E.-M., *Au seuil de la clinique infantile*, érès, 2013.

12 Strasbourg Conference 2004, *Françoise Dolto et le transfert, dans le travail avec les enfants*, érès, 2005.

13 Jablonka, I., *A History of the Grandparents I Never Had*, Stanford University Press, 2016, p. 123

14 Billeter, J.-F., *Études sur Tchouang-tseu,* Éditions Allia, 2004. (TN: My translation.)

15 Wittgenstein, L., *On certainty*, Wiley Blackwell, 1991.

16 Arasse, D., *Take a Closer Look*, Waters, A. (Trans.), Princeton University Press, 2013.

Chapter 2

Clinical Work
Narratives and Scenes

"Spirits quenched by tears, hearts misunderstood [...] children neglected, exiles innocent of wrong, all ye who enter life through barren ways, on whom men's faces everywhere look coldly, to whom ears close and hearts are shut, cease your complaints! You alone can know the infinitude of joy held in that moment when one heart opens to you, one ear listens, one look answers yours. A single day effaces all past evil."

Honoré de Balzac, *The Lily of the Valley*.[1]

The children we will speak of here had been entrusted to the Aide Sociale à l'Enfance (ASE), France's equivalent of Child Protection and Welfare Services. The ASE had placed them in nurseries.

The system in which I carried out my work was composed of three interconnected institutional bodies.[2] They function as follows:

The first level is the Juvenile Court, charged with child protection. The judge who presides over a hearing issues the order to place the child; the child and his family are free to attend this hearing (but various unpredictable circumstances can prevent the child from attending). The placement order is usually for six months, and is renewable, unless the child's return to his family is foreseeable.

DOI: 10.4324/9781003672791-2

The second level of the system, the ASE, has an administrative and social function. Since the decentralisation legislation was passed in 1982, the ASE is a departmental agency. It employs educators, social workers, psychologists and administrative personnel. The educators and social workers representing the child and his family are charged with devising a plan – for instance, the child's placement. The payer manages the financial aid involved, including payment for psychoanalytic sessions (until 2012). Today, they are included in the budget of live-in facilities, increasing their decisional independence, but forcing them to make cuts in other areas.

The third level of the system is comprised of the living facilities offered to the children: foster homes, nurseries, residences, shelters.

As for the placing of babies in infant care homes, this usually occurs in a situation considered urgent, immediately after the situation is reported. Sometimes the placement is made directly by the Brigade for the Protection of Minors, for an observation and treatment period. This is the period needed to assess the child's possibilities – psychoanalytic consultations are included – to develop a "life plan" (depending on the parents' real capacity to take the child back and raise him, or to be present in his life while he is housed elsewhere, and also depending on what housing options the ASE can offer). Children who are placed are not cut off from their families; constructing emotional ties between the child and his family is an important concern. A decision is made about the frequency and form of visits; sometimes, qualified persons (psychologists, social workers, educators, infant home nurses) act as mediators in decisions about visits and housing. The parents and the personnel must abide by their decisions.

It is at this third level that requests for consultation are made. They must be supported by Social Services and sometimes by the Court, in extreme cases.

Françoise Dolto conceived of and set in place, with the team at the Antony infant home, a physical and symbolic support system for children, a system that respected their family ties and created an opening for psychoanalysis as a possible space of encounter, where their distress could be heard in ethical circumstances protecting all those involved. By enabling the emergence of subjects in possession of their individuality, psychoanalysis can claim to serve society by helping to prevent dysfunctions leading to ill health and hospitalisation, confinement in psychiatric hospitals or imprisonment.

In my case, the psychoanalytic work was done with babies born in families so dysfunctional, so broken, so destroyed, that all that remained for these infants was to be integrated into the "human family"; psychoanalysis could help them emerge as fellow citizens.

This inheritance was the foundation on which my work was carried out in several infant care homes. This psychoanalysis was and still is practiced in conditions of urgency. Its aim is to avoid early developmental disorders and malfunctions which produce serious neurological and psychic damage. Today, we understand the importance of the first bonds in the construction of the baby's personality and his brain development. We know that neuronal connections develop differently depending on relational conditions in the baby's environment: "The brain is the result of a double action exerted by our genes and the permanent changes produced by a subject's history".[3]

Invitation to Enter my Office

A few details are needed to describe the physical environment in which the sessions took place. Some children were seen in a CMPP, a Centre called "medico-psychological-educational" in France. The space used in the Centre had not been intended for sessions with infants, but rather for consultations with children between 3 and 18 and their families. An extension of the premises was requested and approved. My workspace was a small room with a large desk in the middle; there was also an armchair for me and two chairs facing each other. On the desk, there were sheets of paper, coloured crayons, modelling clay and balloons to blow up. On the linoleum floor, there were cases containing toys. Across from the desk there was a sideboard for things that had to be stored. A French window opened onto a garden; we were on the ground floor. There were no cushions and no carpet.

I saw other children at my office, which was more comfortable. There was no large desk, but there was a large carpeted area allowing us to be on the floor together. There was also a couch for the babies to lie on, and a table of the right height for a small child.

I will describe my work with babies less than 1-year-old, whom I saw for a consultation only or for treatment of short duration. Then I will discuss a baby whose analysis lasted a year and three months. Finally, I will present older children, between 18 months and 2 and a half years, and I will describe productive moments in their therapy. My role did not include treating the parents, for whom therapy was available; nor did I conduct parent-infant psychotherapy. My task was to uncover the children's endangered potential by offering them, in the psychoanalytic situation, a sphere of availability from which to take what they needed to set out on the path of their lives. We worked together long enough to unlock their potential.

When a baby is well, he shows it. He asserts himself, asks for things without being tyrannical, complains when he feels ignored. He can be consoled, his heath improves, he takes pleasure in eating and sleeping, plays with other babies and makes friends with some and he is comfortable with his parents during visits.

The duration of my work with a baby depended on the plasticity of the baby's condition, and this plasticity depended on his age: before 6 months, there is great plasticity. Therapy duration also depended on how long the baby had lived in his family before he was placed.

I will use the first person throughout my narration, to make the explanation of my method easy to understand. The central thread is my attentiveness to what I experience. It is the helm which guides the process. What I experience is what the patient makes me experience. The feeling is his, but he does not yet experience it himself; he must go through me to gain possession of himself. I give him back his own experience. Often, my awareness of it proves to be enough.

I will describe sessions, narrate incidents and scenes. Certain facts of the babies' histories have been changed, as have all the names of the children and the infant home workers; the latter are designated using initials only. In my comments, I will try not to minimise the strong impact of certain phenomena, so as not to blunt their sharpness, not to reduce their wonder by seeming to understand too quickly, not to turn them into mere explanatory facts. All the children presented in this account were touching. Their confidence made me their witness; they came to me looking for the words that would give them access to living. A baby does not relinquish his need, his desire for recognition; he grabs on to you, he holds you accountable for humanity – his as well as yours – it is what he expects of you.

If no one responds, he prefers to die, physically or psychically. The baby does not set aside his desire for a social bond, his need to be given a voice. The first step is naming, which makes social recognition possible. A birth certificate gives him legal status (he cannot be "undocumented"). At the other end of life, there will be the death certificate and the funeral, a parting ritual as essential as the welcoming among the living – we have only to reread Sophocles' *Antigone*, or see Laszlo Nemes' film *Son of Saul*.[4] For our species, *Sapiens*,[5] as it is often called today, there is something beyond being alive: being human.

That which soothes the child and brings him relief emerges in the session in an *in-between* space. Between what he displays, what he shows, the words I tell him, the words others tell me about him, the words circulating among us. This *in-between* will come to constitute a psychic space in which the baby can regress back to the trauma; his instinctual drive will do the rest.

The Protocol

In a review meeting attended by professionals involved in the care of the baby and his family, it is decided to request psycho-analytic consultation for the baby. The family is informed and asked to give consent, if it is competent to do so. The infant home workers and the psychologists tell the baby that they are concerned about him, and tell him that it has been arranged for him to consult with a psychoanalyst, whose name is specified. No matter how young the baby is, he understands! The decision about what should follow will be made during their meeting. We shall see how, each time, the child reaches out, and how he uses the therapeutic space offered to him. We shall see how a direct contract is established between the analyst and the baby when they are together, with cooperation from the infant home personnel.

The elaborate nature of these preliminaries clearly shows that analytic treatment of a baby separated from his family and placed in an institution requires careful preparation. The analyst comes to constitute the whole environment, the family, the circumstances of the placement. Thus, a shared psychic space between the baby and the analyst is created from the beginning.

Consultations with Babies Entrusted to the Ase

Celim was 6 months old when I met him. He was a solidly built baby bringing to mind an illustration of Gargantua or Pantagruel, with brown curls and porcelain blue eyes. He had been living in the *pouponnière* (public infant care home) for two months. He had created growing concern among his caregivers by his more and more frequent episodes of absence. He rocked back and forth with a blank stare, and stuffed himself with food like a bottomless pit, which explained his excess weight. What was feared was loss of contact, slipping into autism.

When he is introduced to me, he gives me a haggard, unsmiling look, veiled with mist, like a melancholic caress sliding over my face, filled with infinite sadness, and vanishing into the void. This look tells me everything about his impossible attempt to connect with his mother, who became delirious when his gluttonous eyes looked straight into her face – the face of a mother persecuted by the avid gaze of her newborn child. His look spoke of all this: of pain and melancholia, but also of gentleness and love – a gaze as eloquent as that of Jesus's little hand supporting Mary's bowed head in Martin Schongauer's painting *Madonna in Rose Garden*. Celim does not relinquish his desire for an encounter or his offer of love, he does not desert his mother. His gaze caresses, barely touches, because greater intensity, greater passion would be immoderate offer and demand, would become excessive and persecutory. Could one imagine a more delicate lover?

As the sessions continued, he unfroze, warmed by the looks that passed between us while I spoke to him, and his infant home worker provided physical and psychic support. I remember a session in which Celim was crying, on the carpet between A and me, turned towards me in a suspended impulse, and unable either to advance or to give up following his impulse. Suddenly, A, who was watching him closely, exclaimed: "Oh, he is telling you what happened at his last meeting with his mother!" She had been there and was now seeing him reproduce exactly the configuration of the perilous meeting with the mother, where no meeting had been possible, and where his impulse proved futile. The infant home worker understood that he was recounting all this by showing me the scene, expecting me to put it into words. I did this, to free him, to deliver him from the spell of the mother's harmful words, which had ensnared him.

His hands and his gaze sometimes cooperated indolently to help him take hold of an object; but he would quickly drop it, while his eyes lost their focus and his hands became inert once more. Then, he would take hold of things more firmly again. Celim was able to move towards objects, leaving the caregiver's mothering lap. He picked up the objects, then threw them away and went to get them laughing, his gaze, his hands, his whole body finally participating in his action. He had come alive again, he was no longer an inert object.

While we worked together, he had the benefit of my availability and attentiveness to everything that took place. There was also my voice and my facial expression which matched my words; these words described what I saw and what I felt while I connected this with what I knew and was piecing together to construct his history, the story of his mother and him. My words expressed what I imagined his fright to have been when he contemplated this mother who became delusional when her baby looked at her. My words formulated the construction of my thoughts concerning him.

My body was there to welcome him when we were together on the carpet and he played at going back and forth between A's protective sphere and mine. He also had the benefit of A's subtle attention, her arms, her words that connected the child in the session with the child in the infant home and with the child during the meeting with his mother.

He had been caught in the petrified expanse of maternal depression, in a freeze-frame produced by her accusatory tone: "Why do you look at me like that!" she would say when he stared unblinking into her eyes, as all babies do, trying to anchor himself in the maternal other.

Celim had come to me frozen, suspended in time; but he reproduced for me, like a sketch, the inaugural scene of the impossible pleasure of encounter, which could offer him a possible means of connection. An infant cannot develop without this anchoring, this bond with another, established through the eyes, the mouth, the hands, the nose and the ears all functioning together. All "complementary objects",[6] the gaze, the breast or milk, rhythm and rocking, smells and the voice must harmonise. As soon as he is born, the baby needs to connect with a "helpful other",[7] with a "maternal holding environment"[8] where the mother makes her own psyche available to him.

Celim's mouth was a hole which swallowed everything that came near it, no doubt like his mother's eyes, when in her delirious state she had shown him her fear of being swallowed up in her baby's gaze. But for me, the light touch of this gaze, which had not given up – a delicate message of sadness – was an appeal, a con-vocation. With it, Celim appealed to me; I was deeply touched by this state of painful drifting of a child denied attachment. Having been placed in the infant home protected him from the destructive impact of maternal delirium. He was still waiting for an encounter that would confirm his humanity.

Fatou was only 3 months old when I first saw her. She was brought to me for "anorexia". She was heartbreakingly small, a tiny ebony jewel; she had arrived at the infant home directly from the maternity ward.

For her, the danger was not loss of contact. She was very present in the relation, but inconsistently, since she refused to be fed. She seemed to feed only on an exchange of words and smiles. There was a risk of neurological damage due to malnutrition… a risk of death. In these cases, there is recourse to tube feeding, but who can know the psychic cost!

Fatou would sometimes refuse the bottle for a whole day, as she did the day of our first meeting. I thought that this baby had something essential to defend by this refusal, and that we had to hurry to understand what it was. Alarmed, the team at the infant home took her to the hospital. After 24 hours, she finally accepted a bottle. She was in the hospital where she had been born. I took this as a sign. What had happened on the threshold of her life?

I only understood it in our third session when, asking for the bottle, she showed me what no one had been able to tell me: I saw Fatou, firmly held in L's arms while the latter tried to give her the bottle. I saw the baby straining her neck, her head turned so that she could keep her eyes focused on me, while I looked at her and spoke to her. Her gaze was disconnected from her mouth, she could only nourish herself through her eyes and her ears, taking in "subtle" but not "substantial" nourishment, as Françoise Dolto used to say.

By questioning some of the hospital staff, I found out that this reaction to feeding had started in the maternity ward, when her mother tried to breastfeed her. As I could imagine because I had met this touching but delirious young woman, while she nursed the baby her voice and her gaze were elsewhere, and even then, the baby barely suckled. Fatou twisted herself out of shape to avoid those eyes and that voice, which she associates with anyone who feeds her. Her gaze grabbed onto me, it appealed to me to save her mouth, which could not come alive because it had been trapped by the breast of her disabled mother. When I saw, understood and experienced everything at the same time, once she had succeeded in making me a witness, the most crucial work was done.

The transformation always occurs when there is psychic contact between the baby and me; my ability to conceptualise what I see, what I feel, is directly assimilated by the baby, who is then given the emotion he had been unable to feel. Fatou was able to give herself an active witness to the fight that split her in two, her mouth and her gaze disconnected. Now, she could be freed of her fright.

The infant home psychologist, who had had psychoanalytic training, lent support to the team to help the baby nourish herself with milk, words and looks at the same time. Trust grew on both sides. The personnel had been caught up in the baby's terror and did not dare to look at her when they were giving her the bottle, so as not to frighten her and not to be frightened themselves. And it continued this way. In very young infants, suckling – vital for life – involves the eyes, the nose and the mouth, all the senses at the same time. If this cannot happen because the mother's offerings – gaze, speech, odour and milk – are disjointed, the baby experiences a pulling apart which endangers his life.

Celim had turned himself into a leaky thing, to be stuffed; he had sacrificed his psyche to his body. Fatou was sacrificing her body to her psyche. Celim needed several months of therapy; he had come to us already paralysed for months by the trauma. With Fatou, a few sessions were enough, since we were still very close to the trauma.

Fleur, a 4-month-old baby, came into the world as an "anonymous birth". These babies could be adopted at 3 months, according to the law in effect at that time (now the age is 2 months). Fleur's adoption was delayed because of a medical problem; she has had oral thrush (candidiasis) since birth. The condition is very painful, especially at feedings. I saw her three times. Her adoptive mother was present at the last session.

We had been told that at the birth the mother covered her ears as she delivered the baby. What was it that she did not want to hear? The baby's first cry? A cry that rose inside her? We also knew that she had insisted on naming the baby, which is rare. She gave her the name of a white, fragrant flower emblematic of her native country, and symbolising beauty and femininity. Giving these flowers to someone says: "I love you". Choosing this first name for the baby suggested a story of love and abandonment.

When I saw Fleur, I was surprised at how easily she related to others, unlike what one would expect. She babbled and smiled, displaying all her charms for me, while someone was telling me her sad story, a story of abandonment. I sensed, I felt an emotional dissonance in myself, in her. I don't know exactly what I said, perhaps I expressed my surprise at this dissonance. My words were addressed to her, they were for her. At the next session, two weeks later, Fleur cried, stormed and raged, screamed without stopping through the entire session; our ears were ringing. But her thrush went away. It disappeared right after the session.

Cries held back for so long! The cries of pain of the woman abandoned by the man? The cries of the mother who was abandoning the fruit of their love? The cries of the baby entering life? We were in the frozen time of the trauma. Fleur's symptom was hindering her adoption, was holding her back, now that the adoption was imminent. Delivery had not delivered her, the moment of her birth remained suspended, as if it had not happened. My perception of her emotional dissonance allowed her to find coherence without sacrificing it to her need for bonds, for love, for contact: she no longer had to seduce to establish a relation; instead, she could dare to wail and scream, to show her anger, her sadness, not worrying about being rejected.

Fred was 6 months old when I first met with him. He was brought to me for anorexia and total apathy. He slept all the time. For the past two months he had refused the bottle; he refuses to be picked up, he wants nothing except to lie in his bed, where he is letting himself die. What's more, he now has bronchitis. All this causes great concern.

A meeting of the staff is held. It is attended by the ASE educator, the ASE psychologist and her trainee, the public infant home manager and N, the infant home worker who is holding the tiny baby, pale and almost transparent, but powerful enough to have brought all these people together!

Several staff members tell me his story; all those present are aghast.

He was brought to the infant home when he was ten days old, just after maternity was officially recorded. The placement was ordered by a judge after a paediatrician, who saw the mother leaving the maternity ward with the baby, alerted the police. He reported that the mother held the baby upside-down, so that he had turned red. Apparently, the mother, who was alcoholic and somewhat "simple-minded", had taken no notice of her pregnancy. She gave birth at home alone, in the bathroom, during the night. The umbilical cord had not been cut when the presumed father found them in the morning. They were taken to the hospital by ambulance.

I was told that Fred had shown many signs of attachment to his mother. He only suckled properly when she gave him his bottles during her almost daily visits to the infant home. When she returned after staying away for a day, he sulked and refused to look at her. I was also told that he loved being given a bath.

During the staff meeting, I felt that a chill was hanging heavily over Fred and me. I looked at Fred, who lay motionless in N's arms. I was paying close attention to him. In the middle of the dramatic tale of his circumstances, I saw him making little restless movements, and I heard small noises coming from him, not even gurgling, but something resembling throat-clearing sounds, as if he wanted to attract our attention. "Oh, he is hungry." A bottle is produced from a handbag and transferred to the baby's mouth. I watch him "drink" his bottle; in fact, he is barely suckling, his mouth is playing with the nipple. I lean towards him and speak to him. I want to dispel the chill, to push away all the crushing words heaped on him. He seems to be trying to remind us, to show us discreetly, that he is there and wants to have his say in all this, after all! "Everyone tells me about the terribly sad things that happened to you. And you, what do you say? You say that you're here, that you want to play. We want to feed you, but you want to speak and to amuse yourself! You enjoy being alive, despite the drama they're describing." What I'm telling him is what I feel: he is alive, but buried alive! He wants joy and everyone around him is sad. The meeting ends.

The next day, the infant home calls to tell me that he drank all his bottles since he came back from the staff meeting. But there is great concern, because now he has acute diarrhoea and risks becoming dehydrated. He is taken to the hospital. There, an attentive doctor who checks his head circumference percentile is surprised to see that it has not increased for two months. Why did it stop expanding two months ago (when the child became lethargic)? What happened two months ago?

I went to see the baby's ASE educator to learn more about this. Very troubled, she told me: "I found this situation so exasperating, this long-term definitive placement, that I asked the mother to sign a statement of relinquishment two months ago". She didn't sign. The infant home personnel knew nothing about this. Neither did the baby... and yet! The depressive effects were immediate and devastating. The mother had been disqualified and the mother-baby relation, which really existed, was destroyed.

In our sessions, during our exchanges, the mouth of the baby became re-erogenised. It regained its function: that of being the erogenous site of the speaking and nurturing relation. Fred made little sounds, as light as soap bubbles, baby sounds, traces of the maternal voice he had heard at feedings at the infant home. Françoise Dolto would say that when the nurturing mother was disqualified, the baby regressed to the place of his underlying security – the foetal state – the time before his birth, before the umbilical cord was cut. But this state was now deathly for him. Our sessions moved him ahead, he recovered his foundation in the maternal element, his continuity of being, his body with its present needs. And his father, who had rejected the baby, now assumed paternity, proclaiming: "This child looks like me, it's obvious he's mine". So Fred left the infant home in the care of his father!

For a few months, until Fred went home, we met every two weeks. When he had made his little throat-clearing sounds to attract attention, and when I responded to them, he came out of his lethargy. Then he found answers through the hospital doctor, and finally he was able to draw his father into a relationship that allowed him to escape the fate prepared for him by his educator.

John was barely 2 months old when I first met him. What did we know about him and his story? A woman who was left mentally handicapped by a head trauma suffered in childhood, and had been adopted in Laos at an unknown age, was living in a phone booth near Place de la République in Paris; her story remained vague and confusing. She was pregnant and was watched over by Social Services, who advised her to go to a hospital to deliver the baby. When her labour pains started, she went to a hospital maternity ward. She was given a room and was left there with her mother. During the night, she gave birth without any medical assistance, and cut the umbilical cord with her teeth. In the morning, she and the baby were found in a pool of blood; there were scratches on the baby's face – made by the grandmother, according to the mother. Had there been a struggle between mother and daughter because the mother had tried to kidnap the baby for child trafficking? This is what the staff was left to suppose.

Had the mother's body staged a crude re-enactment of other traumas from her childhood, of other pools of blood? This was the thought I had. I would never know, and I did not speak of it. In any case, the situation caused great upheaval. The mother was transferred to a residence without her mother's knowledge; the baby was placed in an undisclosed infant home. The infant home personnel, extremely concerned, brought me the baby for a consultation.

The baby is brought to the second meeting by his infant home nurse, who holds him in her arms, and by his childcare worker. He is introduced to me, as it were. They both tell me that he looks off, he "flutters" – meaning that his gaze wanders off towards the ceiling, flutters – and they can't connect with him. This symptom always worries professionals greatly, they pay close attention to it because it signals the onset of autistic behaviour.

The baby is there, lying on my couch on his back, between his nurse who sits at his feet and me at his head, in my armchair. His childcare worker is facing us, in another armchair. At the beginning of this session, after the baby and I are introduced and he is made comfortable, I suffer a sudden memory loss: I have completely forgotten his history! Everything I have been told, first on the telephone and then at our first meeting, has evaporated, it has simply disappeared! I have a moment of panic that must resemble an actor's nightmarish realisation that he has forgotten his lines, just as he makes his entrance on stage. I am also overwhelmed with shame – how can I be so inept! I feel very guilty and disqualified. All these psychic states manifest themselves in quick succession, like in a dream sequence. I am clearly in a state of altered consciousness. What will help me make contact with him, talk to him, now that I have lost all the words that could have connected us, that I could have used to construct a story intended to put an end to this baby's distress? I take some time to quiet my inner turmoil, to accept my forgetting, to pull myself together. I can only rely on the reality of what I perceive. I take a deep breath… I look. I look at him. I look at him and, now that my panic has vanished, I can see a sweet little baby – not yet 2 months old – a chubby-cheeked little Buddha whose gaze flutters somewhere on the ceiling. Leaning over him, not looking at him anymore but seeing his wandering gaze out of the corner of my eye, I whisper in his ear while I think out loud for both of us, for we both need something to hold onto. I think about what could have happened at his birth to make him unable to find a place to hold onto, to attach his gaze. I am now with him in what he feels, for I myself have no anchor and no language, I am deprived of the words that create filiation, the words that could tell a story. Can forgetting offer a state of receptivity to encounter? Certainly. With adults, forgetting from one session to another is necessary and common. Memory always returns at the right moment. But to forget with a baby who has such a devastating story!

It is then that my memory comes back in a flash as I am talking to him, and that at the same moment he turns his head towards me and plunges his gaze into mine, making his mouth move, opening it, sticking out his tongue to address me, and making little sounds. He drinks me in with his eyes, with his mouth, he seems to suckle on my words; his breath is addressed to me, he sends soft sounds in my direction, he speaks to me! We are now conversing! Deeply moved, I tell him what comes to my mind: "Of course, in the agitation caused by your dramatic birth, everyone rushed to wash you, to warm you, to take care of you, but they forgot to speak to you, to welcome you among us, into the human world!" As always happens in these situations, my words run wild and my thoughts lag behind. I could have added: "They forgot to look at you, to contemplate you, to rejoice, to marvel!"

In fact, without my realising it, in a lightning-quick transference, for the duration of these two meetings he was the stage director who invited me to come on the stage with him, to replay the scene – differently this time. No, that's not right, we'll do it over![9]

We started off by repeating the crime. At our first meeting, I actually neglected to see him; I did not even get a glimpse of him, caught up as I was in the tragic, the revolting, the spectacular picture etched into the words that related his story, as it was presented by his spokespersons. At the second meeting, he himself was, in a manner of speaking, introduced to me. Nothing existed except his presence, the presence of a small living being, perfectly well formed, a flawless jewel whose life force could subvert the power of death inscribed in his story. I can do nothing but see him, look at him. Finally! And therefore, speak to him and welcome him, wonder-struck! Without knowing it, I found myself in perfect resonance with him, in a state of silence, anguish, absence of thought, completely deprived of words that create ties, the missing words that should have welcomed and connected him. My panic was akin to his, but also very similar to that of the hospital staff in the ward where he was born. My deficiency matched theirs, matched their shock and their guilt.

In fact, this block of frozen, engraved trauma: the hospital personnel's trauma, and that of the mother and the baby combined, was passed on to me to unblock, to "uncoagulate", to let the vital flow resume its course by passing through me, awakening my own emotions once I was able to name the baby's. Doing this is an analytic act. The next few sessions freed the baby's ability to express his feelings, to scream, to storm, to shed tears of pain and tears of rage in my presence, for me to see. He had choses their destination: me – the mother – the other, we might say. In "real life", during his mother's taped visits to the infant home, he was able to appeal to and influence this mother, described in the case report as "mentally handicapped following head trauma". When she visited her baby following the session described above, he was able, by screaming and wailing while she held him in her arms, to make her remember lullabies in her native tongue; their sound and rhythm calmed him and rocked him to sleep, to the amazement and relief of the personnel.

This is the third time I have tried to put in writing this sequence of events illustrating my work. I first described it in my book *Accomplir la promesse de l'aube*, and later in an article about transference with babies ("Le transfert avec les bébés"). But its full meaning was not yet explicit. Today, I still remember this sequence of events, I relive it and I am even more rigorously honest with myself. I have to admit that there was a moment when I lost ground, lost my head, became distraught and ashamed, disqualified, guilty of what I then felt was a failure: my unfathomable forgetting. In fact, this very situation is what constitutes the transference, this situation that the inadequately welcomed baby forces the two of us to live in unison, because it echoes what he carries inside him, a frozen mass waiting for a ray of human warmth, waiting to be shared: the dizzying absurdity of a practice-run arrival, a birth only in the flesh.

We can only marvel at the intensity, the violence of this transferential effect, and what it says about the unbelievable capacities of a baby, present from the moment of his birth. They always surprise us – a quintessential philosophical position. What happened was introduced by the baby's reaction to his situation: to the fact that I placed myself in the service of transference, or rather, I was offered up for transference with him, with my consent, by the team who expected this of me, given our common trust in psychoanalysis. The baby was the stage director who put our transference offer to good use. When we make such an offer, we don't know where it will take us. But we sense it. By accepting this role, I exposed myself to experiencing, with the baby, a state of "primitive agony",[10] the distress of an unwelcomed little human being, and I consented to accompany him on a repeat journey into the world, for his sake and mine, both of us finding our way back together.

Here, my thinking converges with Wilfred Bion's concept of the mother's metabolising function, a reshaping function. I am also reminded of Winnicott's primary maternal preoccupation, and André Green's "dead mother complex".[11] And I submit this proposal: that the maternal attitudes these authors described so well only exist as a function of the baby's ability to give rise to them. What I experienced with this baby, as a response to his state of abandonment, in a psychic impetus of intimate "emotional contact"[12] with him, was brought about by both of us in our moving towards each other, a reaction intrinsic to our human condition.

John did not need much more help from me to find his way, to set out on his course. He had been pulled back from the edge of a well, to borrow the image used by Mencius, a Chinese thinker of the 3rd and 4th centuries BC, who formulated the definition of a human being in the negative: "If anyone were to suddenly see a child about to fall into a well and not react accordingly, [he] would not be human".[13] John was rescued by my "primary maternal preoccupation", described by Winnicott; or by my ability to call upon the maternal metabolising function described by Bion – that is, my ability to lend my psyche to the baby, activated in the transference created between us. It was thanks to this ability that I spontaneously bent over him in just the right way, from the side, without looking at him while he was not looking at me, placing only my voice between us and trying to guess, without having the faintest idea, what prevented him from taking hold of his mother's gaze. I was acting under the influence of this urgency, this need to welcome him into the human community. My words sprung from the deepest bond, created to counter the adversity surrounding his birth. The same words also served to separate us, since he was able to use them to connect with those he needed: first of all, his mother, to whom he became able to appeal during her visits, and other helpful people who looked after him at the infant home. My reward was a surplus of humanity.

I was always tense while I waited for the babies to arrive for a session, but the tension disappeared as soon as we were together in the session. It was replaced by a state of joyful pleni-tude when the session was over and it had been productive. At such times, I had the feeling of being perfectly in my place; for a moment, I had the fleeting certainty of being a human being perfectly equal to another.

Benoit was 11 months old when he was brought to see me. He could not sit up alone or stay sitting without support. He could not stand up. He seemed to lack a spinal column, although medical exams revealed no anomaly. A consultation with me constituted a last resort, and I was spared the need to consider physical dysfunctions.

I was told that the baby's parents suffered from alcoholism, and the mother had not been able to abstain from drinking during her pregnancy. The father tried to commit suicide. They were both in despair at the idea of having a child, given their deplorable condition – a child they are unable to "bring up". This expression, with its multiple meanings, attracted my attention.

As usual, I was struck by the child's living presence, despite his sluggishness – a presence that seemed to say only one thing: I am here, let them say what they want, I am just waiting for you to be my interlocutor. I see that he is a beautiful baby: that is, he shows no signs of foetal alcohol disorder. I feel that his appeal for my trust is urgent; he is telling me it's urgent that I believe in him. His need for an encounter and for trust calls out for my response. I am connected to his vital life impetus.

At the following session two weeks later, he is laughing, tri-umphant, sitting up straight on M's knees and pounding his fist on the table! Look how I can hold myself up, he seems to tell us now. During this second session, his mother telephones. She thanks me warmly, she is very grateful to me for having helped her child to recover, and she promises – to whom is she making this promise? – to start detoxification treatment. I can hear that she is happy and relieved; a great weight has been lifted from her, the same weight that prevented Benoit from holding him-self up: the weight of her guilt about having hurt him by drink-ing while carrying him.

The parents were convinced that their addiction to alcohol and their desperate situation had harmed their child's health. They had abandoned their pride and dignity – the dignity that holds people up — they had sacrificed a sense of their personal value. As a result, their baby's symbolic spinal column was flagging, declaring defeat.

Once I understood this, I was certain that trusting the baby was the right thing to do.

I first saw Carlo when he was 7 months old. He was brought to me after a "suicide attempt". His father had killed himself in the first months of the baby's life. The mother, who had no family in France, kept the body in the room for several days, until the family arrived and arranged for a burial. Neighbours in the building alerted the authorities, complaining about the odour. At the infant home where he was living, Carlo threw himself over the bars of his crib and broke one of his limbs. He was still wearing a cast when I saw him. The accident had taken place after his mother left at the end of a visit to the infant home. The mother was very angry, refused her consent to placing him in foster care, and wanted to take her son home. The children's judge decided that the baby should go back to his family.

My work with Carlo ended soon afterwards, when he was 9 months old and went home. When he left after his last session, the pestilential odour of faeces in my office was so strong that I could not see other patients there for the rest of the afternoon, even with the windows wide open! It was only in the aftermath that I realised that he left me the smell of decay, no doubt the same smell his father had filled the house with before his body was removed.

Could this have been his last and only memory of him? Could it be that the baby had actively produced the faeces to leave me with the olfactory trace indicating the constitution of a lost object representing the father? Was this possibly the somatic representation of a loss? We know that the sense of smell has lent its name to the rhinencephalon, a part of the brain essential to the survival of mammals, due to its major influence on mnesic processes. Was this an illustration of the fact that this memory is needed by the young of the human species to construct themselves?

This baby had opened the door to looking into many fascinating possibilities!

Aminata is 4 months old when I first see her. She has a haunted look that frightens her caregivers. Her skin is an unbroken surface of eczema resistant to all treatment. No smile lights up her face, and her huge black eyes stare at you without blinking.

An assistant tells me: "She has Picasso's expression in her eyes!" Yes, Picasso looking at *Guernica.* She looks at us with a piercing gaze. What does she see that we don't? Hell, no doubt.

She was brought to the infant home directly from the maternity ward. After delivering the baby, her mother was placed in a psychiatric hospital in a catatonic state. The delivery was violent – raw flesh, exposed entrails. Here again, the body stages undisguised horror.

We know nothing. The mother is unable to speak. She is helpless. Little by little, as she emerges from her torpor, she starts to recount what happened. The war, massacres, collective rape. Her life was saved by her father, an influential man who was able to put her on a plane to France, pregnant.

Fear crosses the placental barrier and is stored in the tiny body that frightens us. We are afraid of her fear, we share her invisible vision of horror. I hardly did anything more than be a witness and supply words to talk about war, fright and the paradox of being born in the midst of savagery.

We worked together before she left me to go into foster care, unburdened enough and endowed with a great ability to make herself loved. As our sessions went on and as her mother's condition improved, her tension diminished and she softened. But she remained serious, with the graveness of an old person looking upon death.

Samira is 6 months old when she is brought to see me. She has been in the infant home three months. She is always sad, never smiles and cries a great deal – this is what I was told over the phone. She is so rigid that it is difficult for anyone to hold her in their arms. She does not sleep or eat well. Everyone is on the alert, fearing a loss of contact with this baby whose parents have serious emotional problems. The infant care workers are distressed by their inability to offer her nurturance. They decide to bring her to me. The psychologist at the infant care home called me to tell me about Samira, and I agreed to see her.

The initial meeting takes place outside my building. L, the nursing assistant, and the Unit Director are there, searching for the door code. We know each other, they have brought other children to my office before. I know that they come hoping that talking with me will help them make sense of what disturbs a child. Now, the work started as soon as they thought of bringing Samira to see me. And they arrived so early that I felt as if I was late, and shared the guilt they felt at their helplessness, no doubt just as the mother did, and who knows who else.

I bent down to look in the stroller and I had a shock. I saw a baby all curled up, with a grey complexion and knitted brows: the wrinkled, closed face of an old grouch. She gave me a quick glance, then her eyes held mine. I told her my name. Samira and I were introduced. I told her that we were going to see each other in a few minutes in my office.

The second meeting takes place less than ten minutes later (we cross the lobby, take the elevator), at the appointed time. When I open the door of my office, Samira is sleeping soundly.

- She fell asleep right after you spoke to her.
- Very well, let's let her sleep. She needs it after all this effort: coming to see a stranger! Now that she has seen me, she must be reassured and can sleep soundly. Tell me about her.

They tell me what they know – fragments: about the mother's mental illness which caused her to experience extreme episodes during her pregnancy, when she stopped taking her medication; about the fact that she has not visited the baby in the infant home. The placement was made after the baby was hospitalised at the father's request. During his visits to the infant home, he will not put his daughter down for a moment; but she cries through the entire visit.

While I am being told all this, Samira is sleeping in L's arms, with her face turned towards me. I am looking at her while I listen. Suddenly, I no longer hear what is being said because what is happening before me is so intense that it captures all my attention. Samira opens her eyes slowly; her veiled gaze embraces the first Morning of Creation! She smiles. Words spring to my lips, words of welcome, words to praise her beauty – because what I see is truly a little marvel of life. How right her parents were to dare to accomplish their desire for a baby, despite their serious problems! She babbles, she smiles and so do her caregivers, happy and relieved to see her like this – it's never happened before!

I start to play a game with her, using a balloon (it's the toy I prefer for playing with babies). But she soon tires of it and starts to cry. She doesn't know what to do with this object that falls on her, that comes too close. I think of her father's face, his body – also too close – during his visits to her, about which she seems to be telling me. I tell her that she can push the object away – the balloon or her father, whichever one she chooses – with her feet or her hands, or both. And I end the session.

Third session, two weeks later. The same sequence is repeated. I open the door: Samira is sleeping, her face calm now. I am told that she fell asleep outside my building again.

She wakes up just as before. She invites me to replay the scene, to erase once again the memory of her failed arrival into the world.

This time we connect quickly. When we play with the balloon, she concentrates, doesn't cry, blinks, bats her eyelashes and closes her eyes when the balloon comes towards her. She has found the answer all by herself. And I had not thought of it: the closing of her eyelids, like the fall of a curtain, stops the object, makes it disappear, even before her hands or her feet do. Her expression makes me laugh, and that's unusual. I praise her for having found, on her own, this way of protecting herself from the approaching balloon.

Z, another nursing assistant, tells me about Samira's progress, but says that during the weekend she was very sad. Everyone tried to console her, but nothing helped. She can't bear to see an unhappy baby, Z tells me with tears in her eyes.

Fourth session, two weeks later. This time, it is L who brings Samira. She is awake, smiling, completely alert. With the baby comfortably ensconced in her lap, firmly in her place, L brings me up to date. "Samira is doing well, she plays with the others, she has friends, she can defend herself, and she laughs." L tells me a totally different version of the weekend episode of sadness, which she witnessed as well.

She saw this sadness as an appeal to others, not as withdrawal from them. She saw Samira glancing at her out of the corner of her eye, but when L approached and spoke to her, the baby became remote and made her face expressionless. We both understood that Samira had used her to attract and push away another person, a little like she did by blinking and closing her eyes to push back the balloon in her game with me, playing a game of presence-absence using only her glance, only her facial expression. What intelligence and resourcefulness! She no longer needed me, we could say good-bye to each other.

It was only after we separated that I met her ASE educator, who had the child's and the family's Social Services file. We looked through it together. The educator had noted that the mother suffered from depression and anxiety, and was given to projection and interpretation. She had looked at her newborn and said: "Look how unhappy my daughter is, she doesn't smile, she sleeps all the time!"

The absence of smiles and prolonged sleep, characteristic of newborns, were interpreted by the mother in a delirious projection of her own depression as: "She is an unhappy baby". This initial maternal pronouncement had constituted an identificatory nomination: "Samira, the unhappy baby". She had needed my accompaniment for a while, to break free of the spell that cast her in the role of an Unhappy Sleeping Beauty.

In these scenes, we witness the baby's first "I", when he escapes the absolute hold of the maternal word, and we are dazzled!

The Treatment of Yannis, a 10-Month-Old Baby

I will now describe a treatment that lasted a year and three months, a long time for a baby – at the end of which he had become a little boy.

Yannis suffers from constant somatic problems: diarrhoea, projectile vomiting, otitis, as well as relational difficulties. He rocks back and forth in his bed, especially in the evening but also in the daytime, even if someone is with him. He is almost expressionless; he is passive and isolated.

During a review meeting attended by Yannis' caregivers and by his mother, it was decided to request a consultation with me. When I first saw him, he was 10 months old and had been living in the infant home for three months. What I do and why he was brought to see me was explained to him. I introduced myself and the others did the same. Yannis was accompanied by one of the nursing assistants from the infant home and by the head of his unit. Afterwards, he came with any assistant (the one on duty on the day of his appointment), as long as he needed to be carried. Later, when he could walk, the assistant came in with him or stayed in the waiting room, depending on the child's preference. The driver of the institution brought them to my office and took them back.

Yannis is a beautiful mixed-race baby, with caramel coloured skin, brown curls, black eyes that are alert but sombre, serious and a little sad. He has a set smile and his movements seem arrested. He is a well-behaved little boy. During the visit he remains sitting on the floor, next to M's chair, where she placed him when they arrived. He hardly moves, doesn't touch anything, and only gives me his serious smile. I am told that he can't stand on his feet yet, but I feel he wants to stands, since he stretches his arms towards the wall, possibly looking for support.

On the day of the visit, I learn that Yannis is officially recognised by his French mother; his father is not European. He only saw the child once, for a week-end, when he was a newborn. The mother wandered from women's shelter to women's shelter during her pregnancy, and afterwards with the child. She was in conflict with her own mother. The last shelter where she stayed asked for temporary removal of the child and his urgent placement in an infant home. He inspired great concern.

This had happened three months before I first saw him. Two months after he arrived at the infant care home, the Court ordered six-month placement, in the mother's absence. After this, she no longer came to visit the child – although her visits had been very frequent before – perhaps to show her disagreement with the Court's decision, or her discouragement. She opposed the decision.

Since mid-November, the child was doing better. I noticed that this coincided with the Court's decision, which protected him from being exposed to maternal anxiety. He was also told that he would be brought to see me; his mother was informed of the upcoming session and came back shortly beforehand.

Based on information from Social Services, we believed that the cost of the sessions was covered by the mother's Social Security. But her coverage had expired and the Child Welfare inspector was reluctant to pay for the sessions. Yannis' mother was very insistent in her arguments to convince her. She was very concerned about her baby, and looked favourably on the work we could do together.

After the first session, where I had not interacted with him and had only asked for details about the case, I told Yannis that I wanted to see him again, and that I would write to his mother to ask her to meet with me. I scheduled a meeting in two weeks, with agreement from the nursing assistant. At the next session, he came with M, who sat down facing me, a little sideways. She put him down on the floor. This time, he slid over towards the wall and, leaning against it, patted and scratched the wallpaper. The holes in the electric outlet attracted his curiosity: a place of connection.

M told me that after the session Yannis cried when he woke up from his nap. He did not call out, he just sobbed. He only calmed down when they picked him up. I told Yannis that I understood he was suffering, and I offered to see him every two weeks to talk to him and try to help him.

Some time passed because of the Christmas holidays. At his session on January 3, Yannis stands up alone, leaning against his favourite wall. He gives me a triumphant look. He wiggles and jiggles on his feet, jubilantly. I am as happy as he is, and I tell him so. He then asks to sit on M's knees, and draws two faint spirals. M confirms that his motor development has progressed.

On January 16, Mrs. T., Yannis' mother, was present at the session. This would be our only meeting, intense and trying. I was overwhelmed by her volubility, but her verbal diarrhoea proved to be very productive for our work and we reaped its benefits subsequently. I am seeing her and her baby together. She is a beautiful young woman, about 20, tall, looking serious and mature. She keeps her head bent forward, so that her face is hidden behind the curtain of her long hair. She is wearing an outdated pullover and worn grey pants, unselfconsciously. Her tension is palpable. I can tell that she is sensitive, intelligent and very afflicted. She sits down across from me, squeezing Yannis between her body and the desk, encircling him, immobilising him. She is obviously overflowing with emotion and she starts speaking feverishly, plunging into our session head first.

She tells me about the baby's father at length, giving his name. "Yannis is like him, he is always sick." Yannis was a wanted baby – I say to myself that this man must have told her what she wanted to hear, in order to please her: "I will give you a child" – but as soon as she was pregnant, he became violent. He hit her with a belt across the stomach.

I notice that Yannis rocks back and forth when she talks about her pregnancy. When she describes the father's violence, he puts out his hand to take up a crayon, like he did so successfully last time. She gives the little hand a hard slap impatiently; he draws it back at once, as if he were at fault.

This scene – crucial to the session – leaves me speechless, almost in tears. I make an effort to control my own violence and avoid saying hurtful things to this mother. I could have told the child: "You see how worried your mother is that you might cause mischief with your hand". But I was unable to say anything. Instead, Yannis was exposed to my own fear in response to his mother's, and to my shock at witnessing her violence. This fear found an echo in my innermost being, resonating unbeknownst to me, with the frightening experience of the spanked baby I had been. But at the time I was unaware of this part of my history.

Yannis almost died *in utero* at 3 months, as a result of his father's violence. His mother was hospitalised. When she was released, she wandered in the city, often sleeping in metro stations. She was living at a friend's at the end of her pregnancy. When she was eight and a half months pregnant, she haemorrhaged and was taken to the hospital. Delivery was difficult but normal. She breastfed Yannis for four months. He started to rock at 5 months, after he was weaned and after they moved away from the baby's first home. His mother tried to return to her mother's home, but they fought and apparently the mother asked her to leave. This forced her to go to a neighbouring mother-child shelter, where the baby's condition deteriorated severely.

She doesn't want the father to see the child, because of his violence. In any case, she thinks he has gone back to his country to marry. "Later, when he grows up, I'll tell him." I point out that he is there and can hear her. She speaks very quickly, without stopping for breath. She goes on to say that she is happy Yannis looks like his father – which tells me that he is a handsome man. She says she knows that what she says about his father is important. She tells me she loved her own father very much but he died when she was an adolescent. She had said to her mother then: "If only you could have been the one to die first!" This gives me an idea of what the mother-daughter relationship had been at that time, which is not very far in the past. She says that she has only brothers. Her mother "threw her out" with her baby, because his father is "a foreigner". She adds that her father was not racist.

When she spoke of the death of her father, the baby's grandfather, Yannis started to scream, covering his ears with his hands. Impossible to say another word, too much is too much! I am forced to put an end to the meeting, with all of us feeling very uncomfortable. I feel that I have not conducted this session, but was subjected to it, crushed by what had accumulated, prevented from thinking by the verbal outpouring of the mother and her anxiety, from which I could not protect the baby.

At the next session, M tells me that Yannis slept for hours when he returned from the last session: so my exhaustion had been shared! He had not been sick since, his motility is progressing, but he also has great fits of anger if his caregivers don't feed him quickly enough, if they don't pick him up… He even vomits when they put him down; they then have to pick him up again to change him, much to his delight.

Vomiting seems to be his way of asking for constant physical contact, perhaps as a way of remembering his mother before the weaning and the separation from her, when she was breastfeeding him and always held him close (as I had seen her do).

This time, I find him very isolated, engaging in perseverative behaviour, fixated on handling the same object, busy with M's handbag on the floor, playing with the strap, in which one of his feet is caught. When he leaves the bag to go off a little way and explore, he suddenly has trouble breathing. I point out to him that separating from the caregiver's bag brought on his breathing difficulty.

I imagine a hindered birth scene in which the birth is held back, separation from the placenta and the umbilical cord is not taking place, sticking together persists, there is fear of going out into the hostile, unwelcoming world.

On February 27, I learn that Yannis' mother has changed her attitude: she is no longer vindictive but, on the contrary, cooperative. She is seeking advice... and Yannis has stopped vomiting. Now, the infant care home seems to be good for the mother and the baby. Seeing this, I propose a symbolic payment in exchange for a session: a pebble – which he never brought me.

On March 13, I am told that he has let go of any support, and walked without help just before coming to the session. Is this his response to my earlier incitement for him to express his desire? He is 13 months old. He comes, walking through the corridor all the way to my office, slowly, shifting from one leg to the other. I praise him and encourage him. In my office, he hardly moves, takes no initiative and sits in a corner, with a slight smile on his face.

On April 3, C tells me that yes, he walks and moves around, but his fits of anger, his screams and his crying cause great concern. Only his pacifier seems to comfort him.

I tell Yannis and C what I suppose: "Since he is walking, he is no longer his mother's baby. His mother has lost her baby and it's hard for her". C confirms that the mother is annoyed with her son's progress, that instead of being proud of him, she seems to forget that he can walk... and she even seems to forget him altogether, considering that they have not seen her for some time.

Later, I learned that at that time she was pregnant again.

On May 2, Yannis takes a long time to reach my office, swaying back and forth from one foot to the other. He is doing better. He is happier, he wants to play a game where we exchange objects: I give to you, you give to me. I talk to him about his pleasure and mine at giving and taking. I say that it's good to have someone to give to and to receive from.

He is less reluctant to leave M's side, but he stops what he is doing very easily, he lets go easily of whatever he is holding, seems not to hold on to anything and does not even look at the things he drops – and all this goes on in silence. I say: "Did you see where the crayon went when it was not between your fingers anymore? It's on the floor. You dropped it, you can pick it up".

On June 13, I am told that he has given up his pacifier once and for all. He babbles a little. He is acquiring manual dexterity. In the sessions, he comes and sits in a chair facing me, and plays delicately with modelling clay, breaking it into crumbs, and with crayons, with which he draws tangled up lines, fragmented, a little squished together, formless – as if they were broken up as well.

As the sessions continue, Yannis clearly makes progress, but I don't see evidence of an inner spring for his actions. He does not throw objects away from him to go and bring them back afterwards. Objects fall out of his hands, which do not hold on to anything. Previously, this had been true of his bodily functions: he did not hold on to his food, or his stool, which was loose and watery, and is still more or less soft, I am told.

The process needed to constitute the object, the outside and the inside, presence and absence, seems to be lacking. The interplay of the opposites "throw away – take back", inherent to psychic development, has not been set in motion; the engine is idling.

I saw the father's sadism as a frenzied attack of the superego upon the real child, conceived in phantasy with a forbidden woman (not Muslim, not chosen by the family), who must be destroyed. I saw the maternal grandmother's violence as a settling of accounts motivated by jealousy, or as reverse Oedipal envy. Could it be this hate-filled attitude of the grandmother towards her only daughter – "Mirror, mirror on the wall / Who's the fairest of them all?" – that made the young woman pay so dearly for her desire to have a child? Of course, I kept these thoughts to myself.

It is clear that this baby's vital, necessary aggressivity is blocked. His birth in the midst of all these unchained feelings, this instinctual frenzy, seems to have paralysed his vitality, his joy, his active desire to taste life fully.

At this point, the therapy was interrupted by the summer holidays. I saw Yannis again in September.

When I went into the waiting room to get him, his face expressed delight, but he was reluctant to come with me. He stood in place and even walked backwards. What clearer way to illustrate two opposing desires? His happiness at seeing me again – his desire to say "yes" to me – and his desire to say "no", to say "I".

He seems happy to see me again, but wants to decide on his own when to come with me. I praise him for affirming what he wants and tell him that I will be in my office waiting and he can come when he is ready. I make myself comfortable and I hear him approaching slowly with C. They come in and sit down. I am told that Yannis has stopped rocking altogether since he sleeps in a low bed without bars. He visits his mother's family: his grandmother, his uncles, his mother's friend. The atmosphere in the family is more relaxed.

Yannis observes me; he is reserved but happy.

On September 26, part of the session takes place on the way to my office. He comes with me when I go to get him, but he stops on the way, touching the plants, retracing his steps, coming back again.

I make another attempt at symbolic payment. That is when M tells me that sometimes Yannis had gathered pebbles for the previous sessions, but did not give them to me (he left them in the waiting room, or in a corner of the corridor, and most often just left them in his pocket).

In my office, for the first time, Yannis stood up on a chair and, holding on to the desk with one hand, he stretched out his other arm towards the box of modelling clay, out of his reach, looking at me and then at M, babbling at the same time, seeming to establish a dialogue between himself, me and M, so as to make a request for permission and for help.

I say that he is asking for our help to reach the box and I push it closer to him. He is very pleased, jiggling up and down on his chair; he breaks the modelling clay into crumbs delicately, then draws discontinuous lines, broken up like the clay.

At the end of the session, for the first time, he is very upset by the separation. He wants to keep one of my big marker pens, light brown – the colour of his caramel skin, and perhaps also of his father's skin – clutched tightly in his little hand. Letting go of this marker pen, which must stay in my office, stirs up strong emotions which he makes an effort to control. He does not scream or cry, but he starts to wheeze, as if he was about to have an asthma attack.

I notice that as he is building relations and starting to speak, separation becomes more painful for him. I feel his pain. At the dawn of his life, there was an irremediable loss, a radical, violent separation, when his parents parted and his father disappeared from his life. Becoming attached, losing someone and feeling pain become merged together.

What happened at the next session, on October 10, left a deep impression on me. He came to my office as usual, stumbling along. He has had a sore throat. I thought that this illness must be related to the stifled crying in the last session. Repressed sobs hurt the throat. I was also told that his stool is soft.

His mother, who is pregnant, apparently said in front of him that she hopes she has a girl, because "girls are not as hard to bring up". I tell him that he may be wanting to please his mother by not being hard... even in his stools! But, above all, I think that his illness was overdetermined: he was (re)living the trauma of the loss of a father he is trying to constitute, to bring into existence. In order to experience a loss and mourn it, the lost object must have existed, representations of it must persist. In the previous session, we saw the role of the marker pen, phallic, able to mark out traces. Yannick also conjured up his father through his illness. I remembered his mother saying: "He is always sick, like his father". It's terrible, after all, to have to bring an object into existence just to be able to feel its loss and keep a trace of it! What enormous psychic work this little being had to accomplish!

While we talk, he sits in his chair making a drawing. But he drops his drawing and throws the crayons away. At last!

He gets up and walks to the corner of the room where there is a trunk with dolls and a stuffed animal. He takes the stuffed animal out of the trunk and tries to take its place; then he pushes away the trunk to put himself in its place. He tries to disappear under the sideboard next to the trunk, and stays there lying on his stomach, one leg under the chest. He is crying: anger and pain intermingle in his sobs, that are like those which escaped him on the day of his mother's visit to my office, when she spoke of her father's death. "… at last, he spoke, / His grief scarcely allowing a path for his voice", says the poet.[14] Like the last time, his crying distresses me. I am unhappy, unable to find the words to soothe him, to accompany him. What should I say first? Should I speak of his anger about his mother's pregnancy and his desire to be the baby in her belly, to return to the womb? Or about the pain of not being able to go back in time, the impossibility of erasing the event which caused the destruction of the father-mother-baby triangle, and the loss of his father.

I try to console him, but his crying continues, making my words irrelevant. For the second time (the first was the session with his mother), I am forced to end the session while he is still sobbing. His cries are deafening, he doesn't want to hear me, he ignores me while he keeps trying to disappear under the sideboard.

At this point, C stands up and lets him know that she is ready to pick him up, since he has made no move to leave. He calms down at once and gives me a dark look. He has had his revenge after all, in the transference!

Afterwards, I understood that Yannis was not asking me to console him. Consolation was impossible. He was asking me to stay with him while he travelled back to the trauma (the violent break-up of the father-mother-baby triangle), to bear the pain and the rage with him, to withstand seeing him suffer without caving in. This was his achievement: to have made me an empathetic witness.

From then on, Yannis presented no more physical symptoms.

On October 24, he was in excellent form, spoke more and more, gave me and C objects, wanting them to be passed between the three of us. C confirmed that he has made much progress since the crisis that arose in the last session.

On November 14, for the first time, we played hide-and-seek in the waiting room. He hid under a chair, stuck out his head and smiled at me; then he pretended he didn't see me, making me disappear. He can make himself, and can make me, disappear, at his will. The rest of the session consists of trips back and forth between the waiting room and my office, with an "I found you!" exchanged when we meet. Now, Yannis explores the corridors on his own.

Perhaps he is enacting his mother's visits to him. He plays her role and I play the role of the baby subjected to her changing will.

On November 28, after a bit of hide-and-seek in the waiting room, he comes into my office and makes a large drawing that fills the space on the sheet of paper. It looks like a musical notation, the Sol key. This time, he gives me the symbolic payment – the pebble – before he leaves.

C tells me that lately he has been asking for her to stay with him when he is going to sleep. This reminds me of our last session, when he was able to explore the space because he knew he could rely on my presence. Today he has trouble leaving me. He holds on tight, squeezes my fingers and doesn't want to let go.

I suggest to C that he should be given as much autonomy as possible, in the reassuring presence of a person who speaks to him, so that he can be independent without feeling abandoned – the circumstances Winnicott connected with the capacity to be alone in the presence of another person.

On January 9 of the following year, exactly one year after the only session where his mother was present, he is sitting in the chair across from me; he takes up his favourite marker pen, the big light brown one, and struggles to pull the cap off. "Ay!" he says, holding the marker in one hand and the cap in the other. It's the first word I hear him speak, after "pas" (in French, a form of "no").

The marker, which seems to represent him, suffered while he was pulling it apart, and he had had trouble dividing it in two.

I talk to him about his fear of feeling pain and causing pain. He comes over to me while I am writing like I always do, and he slaps the hand which is writing! Then he takes a pencil and writes on the same page. "Yes, we were both afraid of violence, but now neither one of us is afraid."

This scene takes place one year after his mother slapped the little hand that was reaching for a crayon, while she talked of the blows his father inflicted on her when she was pregnant, blows that he, the foetus in her womb, received as well – blows of which she spoke in his presence, while saying that she didn't want him to know about them... What a memory! I remind him of all this, I talk about his father as I perceived him from his mother's description of events: the hand that can inflict pain, that can be brutal and terrifying, and the separation that is painful as well.

I say all this quickly, as it comes. I too would have liked to protect him from this reality: the father's destructive violence, the blows, the abandonment, the distress. Yannis had experienced this violence, but his mother had denied him access to his own emotion, which remained frozen as long as she negated his ability to understand. She needed to protect the "father image" – no doubt that of her own father. A paradoxical attitude, since at the very moment when she was declaring her refusal (to allow him to learn that a father can be destructive), she was slapping him on the hand, recognising that he could withstand violence, live with it – that he could bear pain. That day, I knew that everything was recorded in his memory.

Indeed, we can suffer and cause suffering. It's part of being alive, part of loving, being attached and becoming detached.

After this exchange, Yannis was at ease and playful in all our sessions. He would sit on my desk, facing me, very close, would give me little playful taps on the hand and feel my nose with his fingers, all the while babbling gaily. The plug, the cap that stopped the flow of life, its inscription, had been removed. The "ay!", uttered and felt, signalled the possibility of existence.

On January 23, he brings a pebble and gives it to me. He strolls up and down my office, giving me big smiles, obviously happy. I am told that earlier, at the home, he was sad. I conclude that he is able to let go of his emotions. During the session, he speaks a great deal. He laughs, provokes me, teases me, he is no longer afraid to ask and to be aggressive, to be alive. I feel he is out of the woods.

On February 6, he is in the lavatory when I go to get him in the waiting room, so I wait for him in my office. He comes in alone, gives me a quick greeting and goes out again. I hear him tell the nursing assistant: "No, no, no". Then he comes back alone. I praise him for his independence. He speaks using new words: "scissors", "daddy", "mommy", "no", "again", "write". He draws with confident, spread-out strokes of his favourite colour.

On February 15, his half-brother was brought to the infant care home, as I learned at the next staff meeting. Now, Yannis can be the big brother. I was given no other information about the baby brother.

On March 13, M tells me that Yannis asked for the potty for the first time; on the same day, I saw him use the scissors skilfully. M says that he is doing very well, that he is proud of his brother, that he laughs and speaks.

This tells me that the wounds caused by the trauma surrounding his birth have now been sufficiently soothed and thought through. I know he can bear a separation without losing his integrity. His vital aggressive drive, oral and anal, seems to be functioning well. His narcissism is restored, now that the father has become a real human being despite his absence, instead of remaining idealised as the phantom of the grandfather.

I decide that I can trust him to continue on his way within the infant care structure and in his family, which has been able to give him his place. I tell him that he has come to see me that day to show me and tell me how well he is doing, and that he doesn't need me anymore.

It was our last session. It took over a year to discover and treat the early traumas suffered by this baby. He had to construct a trusting relationship with me; this took time, given the extremely hostile circumstances in which he was born. He had to trust that his aggressivity would not destroy me, that the object of his libidinal investment would survive the attacks to which he subjected it.

We might have advanced faster perhaps if I had not been stunned by the violence. But it may also be that because his traumas resonated with similar ones deeply buried within me, together we were able to bring about his progress.

Yannis' Drawings

The drawing made on January 3 of the first year introduces the series. Yannis was then 10 months old. It is already clear that this child has enormous potential, as shown by the quality of his presence, his desire to speak and his involvement in our work.

Figure 1

Figure 2

Figure 3

Figure 4

Figure 5

Figure 6

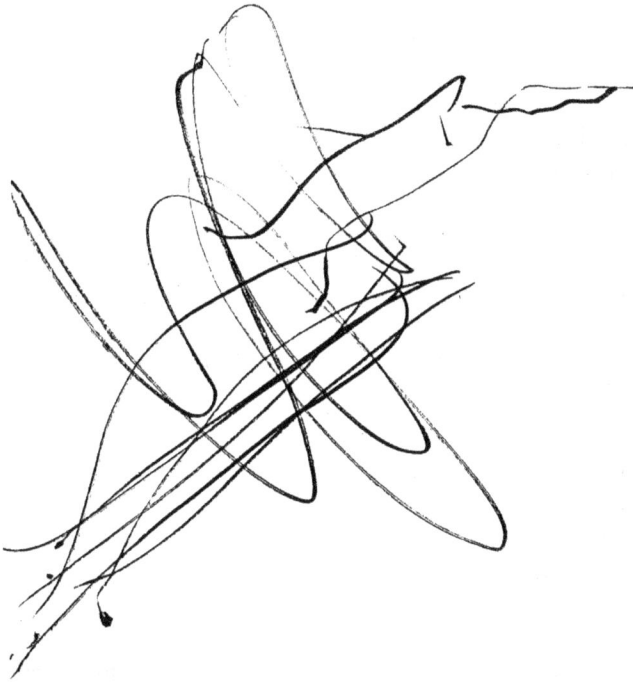

Figure 7

The spirals he draws have life, the strokes are precise; he is discreet, shy. There are two spirals, two speaking subjects occupying the same space.

In the subsequent drawings, the two spirals become more indistinct, until there is only one left, fragmented, broken up, as if to show the effects of so many brutal attempts at separation – their disintegrating effects.

And then we come to the last two drawings. Yannis has consolidated his inner sense of security, he can be alone (in the presence of a helpful other). He has constructed his integrity. In the magnificent final drawing resembling a musical notation, we can see the transformation which took place, liberating a vigorous life impulse.

Productive Moments in the Treatment of Toddlers Between 18 Months and 2 and a Half Years

Let us look more closely at the decisive moments of change in the work with young children. They are no longer infants, they have survived the trauma of their birth, they have started to develop, but the trauma, which creates a gap in the psychic structure, manifests itself in the form of difficulties in their everyday lives, as is the case for adults who consult a psychoanalyst. But the later were able to reach adulthood, while the former struggle on the threshold of childhood.

Nina, 2 years old or thereabouts, was one of my first little patients. She introduced me to the world of children plunged into solitude from the first moments of their lives. She insisted bravely on coming to her sessions alone. She was toilet trained, very independent, a veritable little woman who did not ask for anyone's help; this endeared her to those around her. She was seeing me because she had fits of anger and frustration which resembled rages – a "personality disorder", as some called it. In one of our sessions, when I offered to help her take hold of a box of crayons out of her reach (as she indicated without asking that she wanted me to do), this little girl no longer in diapers started to urinate as she sat in her chair. I saw the urine run down onto the floor and make a large puddle under the chair. She sat with her eyes fixed on me, drinking me in wordlessly, without a sound.

At that moment, she had become (or become again) a baby, the baby she had not been able to be, who was expressing the need to be mothered, to be cared for, to have her body tended to, because now, suddenly, this had become possible. After this, she never wanted to come to the sessions alone. She took pleasure in the real relationship she had developed with her caregiver, opening the path to other relations.

Loïc was 18 months old. He was also living in the infant care home while waiting for a more permanent situation. He was brought to me because he had trouble relating to others and trouble sleeping, as well as behavioural problems – all of which are signs of psychic suffering.

In the very first session, I see that he is torn between two impulses: the desire to be held, as he sits on L's knees, and the desire to leave the circle of her arms and move towards the toys he sees. He is unable to put an end to this "period of hesitation".[15] This scene is repeated at each session, until it becomes torture for me to watch him, with no idea of how to help him stand on firm ground. He cannot leave L's lap and stand up without screaming. The ground seems to burn him and he hurries back and hangs on L's neck, only to repeat the whole thing a few minutes later.

This scene he plays out before me calls for the words that could deliver him at last; delivery is a term designating expulsion from the placenta. But I cannot find the words, the scene leaves me speechless. Faced with his absolute inability to leave encircling arms, as if they were enveloping placental membranes, I cannot think. Finally, I am able to shake off the trance (why, how?) I take a breath, think again and associate using elements of his story of which I have been informed and which I now remember.

He suffered a double catastrophe at birth: first, he lost contact with his mother very quickly, because he was taken to the infant home directly from the maternity ward, where her visits were rare; at the same time, he had to endure the torment of withdrawal, since his mother had been addicted to crack throughout her pregnancy. He had drug withdrawal symptoms despite receiving medical help during the first months of his life. I talked to him about this and he became calm enough to play on the floor.

A young child shows, acts, in order to ask his question, to call forth the words that will give him access to what he experienced, to his experience recognised at last. "This is what psychoanalysis can achieve: to inscribe in an individual's story the segments of time torn out of his history",[16] Françoise Davoine wrote. At 18 months, Loïc acts out the trauma of his birth. This dramatic moment could not be inscribed due, perhaps, to the immaturity of the newborn, but above all because there had been no one there – his mother or any maternal substitute – able to experience it with him.

How can a paediatric nurse or a caregiver in an infant home, who is intimately involved with a child, bear this excessive burden of pain? It's unthinkable. The priority is to put an end to the pain. This is why the child appeals to us, for it is urgent for him to make this excessive pain thinkable, since he has experienced it.

What has been experienced must be made thinkable. Like Yannis in our October 10 session, when he was not asking me to console him, but rather to be able to bear his suffering, Loïc is not asking me to take away his pain, which he has survived, but to recognise it.

Laura is 18 months old. She is brought to see me because she suffers from "persistent diaper rash". The condition does not respond to any treatment. Typical of a newborn, the condition is strange in a toddler like her. She has been living in the infant care home since she left the maternity ward. She is the third daughter in the family, and the only one who never lived with her parents. Her older sisters were placed in infant homes after living in their family for a while.

I don't know what to think and nothing seems to happen, until one day it occurs to me to ask for details about this persistent diaper rash (why and why just then?) I ask that it be described to me. And suddenly I understand. In fact, the rash is not on the buttocks, but on the vulva. I suggest to Laura that she might have believed that she was placed in a facility, abandoned, because her parents wanted to get rid of a third girl, because they wanted no more girls.

At the next session I am told that the rash disappeared immediately after the previous session. And the little girl in my office speaks her first word, addressing herself to me and pointing with her little finger at the garden outside the French door: "Look!" An invitation to look outside together, at the garden, the beauty of the flowers, of the trees, of nature.

Private parts in pain, suffering cruelly, unveiled, calling forth words about her wounded femininity which wants to offer its beauty. As François Jullien writes:

> Only that which is private wants to offer itself and can do so. It is because our "private" parts, as they are called, are the most remote, not to be revealed, to be sheathed and hidden, that they can be uncovered and presented to the gaze of the Other, and that exposing them is in itself a gift.[17]

Now, the private could be covered and the little girl could marvel, as we looked outside together, at the wonder of the garden offered to our gaze. What happened? Did it happen because I addressed her as a subject, a girl, recognising her in her singular suffering femininity, from the position of my own singular femininity? Because her suffering echoed mine – a second daughter, her girlness not desired, arriving at the end of the Second World War, awakening the pain of the death of the men lost in the previous war, and underscoring their absence? Another girl!

Joseph is 2 years old when he is brought to see me, because he has a way of being forgotten. He comes with his mother, who lives with her whole family in social housing in a hotel. The family's social worker has come with Joseph as well. At his kindergarten, Joseph makes himself invisible; his behaviour worries the staff and creates guilt feelings: it is not at all professional to forget a child! He puts them in danger of committing a serious fault, and places himself in danger as well.

A number of sessions take place with the mother and the social worker present. I learn that there was pregnancy denial on the part of the mother, with the participation of the whole family, including the father. She went to the hospital suffering from abdominal pain, and gave birth on the steps leading to the entrance. She was delirious for several days before being able to acknowledge her child and become attached to him. She started by saying that he was not hers and she didn't want him. She already had several children and was in the process of separating from the father; their life together was fraught with violence.

Women too can refuse to recognise a child. Could pregnancy denial be the feminine equivalent of refusing the responsibility of paternity, which in the past produced the phenomenon of unwed mothers and illegitimate children? The subject remains to be studied.

During the sessions, Joseph is inactive, remaining practically glued to his mother. I can only contemplate the scene as a silent, helpless witness. One day, I suddenly feel – I don't know why – that I can and that I must see him alone. I ask the two women to wait outside the office. Joseph and I are left alone together. He is standing, playing with two toy cars, making them roll on the table. They crash into each other; in the accident, one of them falls off the table. Joseph goes into hiding, or rather, disappears, slender as a sheet of paper, behind a piece of furniture in my office, that until then I had thought to be pushed up against the wall! Nothing I say persuades him to come out. I feel stuck, ignored, guilty of doing this to him, like the staff who forgets him, guilty like his mother who denied her pregnancy. He stays hidden, stuck to the wall, until his mother returns. As soon as he hears the bell, he hurries out of his hiding place and goes to her.

Once everyone left, I finally emerged from my numbness and was able to think about what had happened. Joseph had made me witness and feel what he had experienced in his mother's womb, what he kept playing out by causing people to forget him: how he had hidden, disavowed by his mother; how he hid, incognito, in an incredible position – as we now know to be the case in these situations – stuck to the spinal column. The body too can be delusional.

Has this position saved his life (averted an abortion), in tacit agreement with his parents, who found this way to resolve the aporia of their desire for a child? Had it been the father who wanted this child, the only one the mother did not claim as her own? What I learned much later confirmed this: he brought up the child alone, in his country of origin, in his family (as Fred's father had done). Had he used the mother as a mere surrogate?

At the next session, I was determined to speak to Joseph. But there was no need! He was through with this story, he had only needed to play out the scene in the right place, that is, a place where a perceptive witness could accompany him back to the trauma. When I saw him later, he was laughing, playful, no longer stuck to his mother, active. And he was ready to separate from me.

In each of these three situations, I cannot say how the idea came to me – the idea which suddenly reminded me of the pain of Loïc's birth, which I had "forgotten"; the idea that made me ask for details about Laura's rash, details I had not sought to learn earlier; and the idea that I should see Joseph alone. The idea sprung up suddenly, as if to break a spell, like the inversion of an upward movement, a sudden surge of energy allowing me to find momentum and reverse the process. The idea emerged from an absence of thought. I believe that the prospect of experiencing this absence of thought produced my anxiety before each session.

Patrick is 18 months old. He has been in the infant care home for a long time. He is sickly and so unbearable that it isn't possible – nor is there any attempt made – to find him adoptive parents, although he has the legal status of an abandoned child. No one seems able to propose a life plan for his future.

In his sessions with me, he is very agitated, bursting with anxiety. He can't sit still and I don't know how to calm him. I remember the session in which a change came about. I decide to talk to him, reluctantly, about his conception, his pregnant mother's hesitation about keeping him, and her failed attempt to end her pregnancy. In any case, now he is here alive; he was able to hold on and to be born. I focus attention on what I see: his vitality. That is when an incredible scene takes place: he jumps on me and starts to climb up on my head like a little monkey; he grabs on to my hair and won't let go. I can't find the words needed to make him relax his grip. He only lets go when I say: "It's over". As was the case with Joseph and with Yannis at his October 10 session, ending the session stops the child's "ostensive" behaviour.[18]

At our next session, when I go to the waiting room to look for Patrick, he turns his back to me, looks out the window and says in a tone that is loud and clear: "No pebble, Mommy!" He is stating firmly that he does not have the payment symbolising his commitment to our work together, a payment he had always brought in the past. He doesn't want the session. He knows what he wants, he can decide to separate from his birth mother, what he wants is a mother. I accepted his decision and agreed to end his treatment, much to the dismay of Social Services, left helpless. What happened next? I learned much later that Patrick became so likeable that he was adopted.

Joseph and Patrick made me an eye witness to the tactics to which life can resort to preserve itself.

I saw Jonnah when he was 2 and a half. He has been in a foster home since he left prison: his mother was incarcerated, and he with her, so that they would not be separated. He has trouble sleeping, he is anorexic and, most troubling of all, he rocks back and forth during the day as he sits staring blankly into the void. He also has a strange night-time ritual to prepare for sleep: he strikes his forehead violently with his fist (he has a bump) while he rocks himself and hums a melody resembling (p)in (p)on (p) in… But he establishes contact with others easily.

Nothing much happens. I have no ideas and no particular impressions until one of his educators tells me a very disturbing story. She describes the mother, whom she has just visited at the psychiatric hospital; she was hitting her head against the wall and the educator learned that she was already doing this when she was incarcerated with her 2-month-old baby, in a prison where the sound of ambulance and police car sirens was heard constantly.

I am deeply touched by this woman's distress. I imagine her circumstances and I understand the scenario the child constructed on the traces left by a previous scene in which he took part with his mother. His ritual was put together from remembered fragments of frightening events, but events which took place when he and his mother were together. His ritual served to render her present, to have her with him in moments of solitude, for instance on the brink of sleep – a disquieting moment of separation. Françoise Dolto spoke of the return to an *unconscious image of the body*, an image preceding the separation, a time when the baby's basic security is guaranteed.[19]

After this conversation, now that I carried his mother within me, I was able to talk about her to John in our sessions when he started to rock back and forth frantically. This made the symptom disappear.

This is what happens in analysis with an adult, when the analytic work causes the patient to come upon a ghost in suspended animation, or a scene where emotion became frozen. The analyst's emotion is needed to reanimate the ghost, so that it can finally be laid to rest. But with adults, we do not have elements contributed by a third person.

What we have in the work with children, as I described earlier, is the moment when my ability to think what the child must feel is immediately assimilated by him, allowing him to feel it, although until then it had been left out of his psyche.

Notes

1 De Balzac, H., *The Lily of the Valley*, Waring, J. (Trans.), Philadelphia: The Gebbie Publishing Co., 1898, p. 82.
2 I worked in this system for 25 years. Recently, certain changes have been introduced.
3 Vincent, J.-D., & Lledo, P.-M., *The Custom-Made Brain*, Columbia University Press, 2014.
4 Film, Laszlo Nemes (Dir.), 2015. Based on the book *The Scrolls of Auschwitz*, a collection of testimonies by Sonderkommando members in Auschwitz-Birkenau.
5 Harari, Y.N., *Sapiens: A Brief History of Humankind*, Harper, 2015.
6 Piera Aulagnier's expression. For the newborn, the breast is the "complementary object" in fusion with the mouth, in his inaugural encounter with the world. It is the object of an instinctual drive, a "partial" object, according to Freud, a love object, already the other.
7 Freud's term for the person ensuring the baby's survival.
8 Winnicott's concept.
9 See, on the same theme, my work with Samira, *infra*, p. 000.
10 Winnicott's expression.
11 Green, A., "The Dead Mother", in *On Private Madness*, Routledge, 1996.

12 Latrouite-Ma, M., "Yin and Yang, the Process of Separation in the Infant. A Chinese reading of a *fort-da* passage", *Le Coq-héron*, No. 237, 2019/2.
13 De Bary, W.T., & Bloom, I. (Eds.), *Sources of Chinese Tradition*, Columbia University Press, 1999.
14 Virgil, *The Aeneid*, Book XI, Cambridge University Press, 2020.
15 Winnicott, D.W., *Through Pediatrics to Psycho-Analysis*, New York: Basic Books, 1975, p. XVII.
16 Davoine, F., *Wittgenstein's Folly*, Routledge, 2023.
17 Jullien, F., *De l'intime, loin du bruyant amour*, Grasset, 2013, p. 29.
18 Françoise Davoine's expression, borrowed from Wittgenstein.
19 Dolto, F., *L'image inconsciente du corps*, Le Seuil, 1984.

Chapter 3

Language, Words and The Body

The Appeal and the Address, the Invocation

> *"What is called appears as what is present, and in its presence it is secured, commanded, called into the calling word. So called by name, called into presencing, it in turn calls. It is named, has the name. By naming, we call on what is present to arrive. Arrive where? That remains to be thought about."*
>
> Heidegger, *On the Way to Language.*[1]

I hope that I have conveyed my amazement at the incommensurable potential babies possess, and at the life process regulated by means of language. Momentarily impeded by catastrophes, this process resumes its course, like a river which settles into its bed after being disrupted by a storm. There is enormous capacity for repair.

The word is the hand held out to accompany the baby in his regression back to the trauma, until his own life energy takes over. At an exhibition of Rembrandt's paintings, I saw this inscription: "Rembrandt is the artist who painted the effects of language". Writing has trouble expressing the effects of the spoken word.

What does the psychoanalyst need in order to impart humanity to a baby who suffers? The child signals his distress to his caregivers. These signs of torment, anguish and hopelessness are

DOI: 10.4324/9781003672791-3

calls for help. They are heard by the caregivers, who bring the child to a consultation with the analyst. The message in a bottle thrown into the ocean has been found. The baby has "prior knowledge of a connection",[2] an intuition of the Other. Not without the other – this much he knows. He seems to arrive into the world with an awareness of the reception due to him, by virtue of his human status. He summons, he attributes a task.

Jacques Lacan spoke of an "invocatory drive", saying that invocation connects the one who is appealing to the one who is appealed to; the former solicits and addresses the latter, bringing him into existence through a specific nomination. Invocation implies recognition of the Other and of his inadequacy. The babies we saw were in distress, either because they had not been met by the Other, or because the Other was deceptive, unwelcoming, destructive. These babies were left waiting.

Babies solicit recognition by their father, their mother and the human community, who will inscribe them in their filiation and in the human family, with their specified origin which connects them to the entire human species, until an Other comes into being and can be addressed, "the prehistoric, unforgettable other person [...] the prime originator".[3] Babies await an encounter with a "complementary object"[4] which will awaken their sensory zones and allow them to discover their capacity for experiencing pleasure, as Piera Aulagnier described. The nomination and the encounter are indissociably linked. Without the inscription, the baby cannot encounter the Other, others.

All the babies presented here had parents who experienced great psychic difficulties. The mother or the father, when they were known (and often they were not), suffered from a psychiatric disorder brought on by destructive life events, either in the past or recently. This prevented the encounter with the baby from taking place. But Eros is persistent and the infant continues to invest his energy in the expectation of a future encounter allowing him to begin his life.

The offer to listen, and the words addressed to the baby in response, fulfil this expectation. John's response provides a spectacular example of this. What I told him produced an immediate effect. He received from me what he needed to create a connection and to activate this ability in his mother. Indeed, I learned that during her visit he screamed and hollered so loudly in her arms that, in order to calm him, she remembered a song in her mother tongue, a lullaby from her own childhood. The baby fell asleep peacefully; he had been able to find/create[5] "all that the mother is" and what he needed: her arms, her voice, all of her. Songs in her mother tongue that come into her mouth, and the milk that comes into her breast, are found/created by the baby.

Solitude: Words as an Offer of Help

"When a solitary man suspended over an abyss is a bridge unto himself, he is not equipped to turn around."
Philippe Réfabert, *From Freud to Kafka.*[6]

The solitude in which these little patients have lived (each one differently, depending on his age) forced them to develop a certain autonomy, fictitious but useful to them, and sometimes to their caregivers. But they have become unable to benefit from the mothering they receive, to which they remain indifferent. They have not developed the necessary "space of illusion".[7] Therefore, we must offer our help in the same way as the mother offers the object, letting the baby have the illusion of creating it. We can't help them without their consent; otherwise, the adult's actions would be manipulative, he would be guilty of persecutory omnipotence, and his help would be impossible to receive.

On the other hand, telling a baby right there, in a given situation, that he can, if he wishes, take advantage of the arms that offer to carry him, rock him, console him, and present his cuddly toy, his comforting object, by placing it near him without giving it outright – as I have seen it done with infinite delicacy – to say, but without doing, that he can have help doing what he clearly wants to do: climb up on a chair, get hold of an object or pick it up from the floor, instead of giving up because he could not ask for help – to say words conveying this is absolutely necessary to enable him to turn to a "helpful other". Without such accompanying words, these babies don't know that they can count on us. Because relying on someone is something they have not experienced, they cannot anticipate it. They need the thought and the words of a witness.

In order for them to address the world, to be desiring beings in the world, to take hold of objects, the world and its objects must first address them, objects must be placed within reach by an intermediary, a singular other who introduces them, as it were. Winnicott conceived of a "transitional psychic matrix", a psychic space which is neither the mother's nor the infant's. A "space in between", as François Jullien calls it. These formulations suit me. What the analyst activates in the session is the capacity Bion calls "the mother's transforming function".

To tell a child effectively that he can ask for help if he wishes, one must have experienced this possibility oneself – that others can be counted on, that one can ask. And what the child is told must be true. This is, no doubt, what Françoise Dolto referred to as " speaking the truth". This approach forces adults to forgo so-called natural reactions, in order to encourage the subject and his desire to emerge. Not to rush to help a struggling child, to resist doing something for him – in his place – or to do something when he has not turned to us, or given any indication that he wants help, requires having great respect for the child, being very attentive and patient. To consider the very young child a person is a true psychic accomplishment which will allow the baby to find/create the object presented to him at the exact moment when he desires it.

Not to push a chair towards him, not to help him climb up on it, not to push forward a box of marker pens or modelling clay, not to pick him up to console him, not to help him out of a difficulty, but to simply say, instead: "You can ask for help, your caregiver and I are here to help you", is not at all spontaneous or easy, and can make us feel guilty. But the liberation this produces every time for the child, his pleasure when he asks for help or when he succeeds in doing something by himself, this striking birth of a subject confirms our approach in each instance.

This approach sometimes causes spectacular regression, as was the case with Nina. I have seen babies whose bodies collapse like a dropped sandbag when the trauma is mentioned. Therefore, another person must be there to attend to this collapse in the transference, to make this "letting go" possible. The child's self-concept then develops in the relation with a real person who is present, to whom he had no access previously and towards whom our words, like a helping hand, have guided him.

Language and the Baby

Language, and particularly words, those of the mother as well as those of others who are present, have a strong effect on the newborn. It is common, but always surprising, to discover during a child's treatment, the impact of words spoken at his birth. In *Dominique: Analysis of an Adolescent*,[8] Françoise Dolto spoke of words imprinted "like a recording". Samira was ushered into the world by her mother's words, etched into her body: "See for yourself, she is an unhappy baby, she doesn't smile, she sleeps all the time". Words produce effects and leave a trace. The infant records words, silences, gestures, a manner of holding. These are all components of language. Piera Aulagnier used the term "pictogram" to designate the first inscriptions of the encounter with an Other, which will determine the infant's mode of being-in-the-world, his physiological functioning, his relational capacity. Indeed, babies placed in institutions induce their caregivers to adopt the mode of interrelation to which their mothers accustomed them from birth.

Carrying a child is not "natural". A baby who was not carried well by his mother, who was not protected, who received inadequate holding,[9] does not let himself be mothered. His body stays stiff, tense, unable to snuggle, to cuddle, to let itself go, to trust, because he has been forced to carry himself as well as the mother who could not carry him. The gaze of such a baby wanders aimlessly somewhere near the ceiling.

Fatou could not take in food because her gaze and her whole tense body had had to turn away from her mother's delirious gaze. Celim swallowed food while he sat motionless, like an inanimate object. Yannis sat still, paralysed, his body immobilised by the corporeal memory of being held by a mother who feared his slightest movements, perceiving them as potentially dangerous. These babies remained prisoners of their mother's terrified body and psyche.

Babies who don't let themselves be mothered are a cause of suffering for caregivers devoted to their task. These infants seem to refuse contact with another body, while in truth they are simply unable to experience this contact as being good for them. They have been left with a memory of danger, of lack of safety – a memory transmitted to them by the mother's presence, her body and her gaze. But the caregiver's suffering reveals the child's suffering; she recognises it because it is what prevents her body from becoming present for the baby. This suffering makes a diagnosis: the baby is repeating a behaviour pattern like a broken record.

Part of my work was aimed at supporting the caregivers by correcting mistaken impressions about their charges. Changing the way they perceived the child freed them of guilt feelings and resentment caused by a sense of failure, as if the child was holding them responsible. To think that a baby refuses contact because he misses his mother and the caregiver is not doing the right things is an error. A child who has known adequate mothering has a special tie with his mother and may refuse care from someone else in her presence, to show his loyalty to the love they share. But when she is absent, he accepts care from others because he welcomes pleasure and is able to trust. Trusting is something he has experienced.

Another part of my work consisted of discerning the gap between the offer of care and the baby's ability to avail himself of it, as I have been discussing. My task was to find words I could give him, to be a perceptive witness, a witness who sees and feels the drama inscribed in the body language of a baby who sees and feels the discordance between the languages of the arms, the breast, the gaze, the voice and the words addressed to him.[10]

Like a piano tuner who makes notes resonate in harmony, a psychoanalyst who has acquired perfect pitch listens with a heart-mind-body ear which creates coherence. A remarkable film, *The Story of the Weeping Camel*,[11] tells the story of a young camel that abandons and refuses to feed her calf, whose birth caused her extreme pain. The calf refuses to be bottle-fed and is letting itself die. The camel can only start to nurture it after a musician makes her hear and feel the music of the wind in resonance with the vibrations of her body.

The Encounter: A Paradox – Encountering to Dispose to Attachment[12]

Over the years, through my own experience and acquaintance with certain masters and texts, the knowledge I acquired about child development gave me the certainty that these little beings would not become attached to me. This is useful to know as a general fact, but it does not offset my lack of knowledge about each particular child I meet. Our work together takes place in another dimension, in a sphere prior to that of the usual encounter, a sphere of resonance, a preparatory energy field. I was able to observe this in every case, to my great joy. When the little ones have had enough, when they obtain what they have been looking for, they leave! They make me understand that our work is finished, in the most explicit manner: bodily, by crawling towards the door; by ignoring me and busying themselves with their own affairs in the session; by directing a meaningful look at their assistant, to signal that it is time to leave; by dropping the note with the date of the next session, which I give them because I have not yet understood that it is time to let them go. Now, they drop the piece of paper they used to clutch tightly in their little fists before. They have no lack of means to convey their decision. At times I hesitate because of the team's fear of losing my support. The team has not yet understood either. The child is always ahead of the rest of us.

All these clinical accounts bring to light the essential question of attachment. "A crucial element of rootedness [...] conferring the certainty of belonging to *the human race*",[13] attachment allows the infant access to the other and, at the same time, to his own life, to himself.

Konrad Lorenz, the father of the theory of "imprinting", described the following phenomenon: when he appeared before baby ducks just hatched, the ducklings took him for their mother! They followed him everywhere, as ducklings usually follow their mother. As a result, Lorenz reconsidered what we call "instinctive behaviour", calling it "imprinting" instead.

In the humorous animated film *Ice Age 3: Dawn of the Dinosaurs*,[14] newly hatched baby dinosaurs, already enormous, whose eggs had been adopted by a lazy man, follow the man everywhere, imitate him, take him for their mother. It is pure imprinting!

Things are different for human infants. There is imprinting, or rather marking, by language. But, at the same time, the name which inscribes the newborn in a filiation is his point of anchorage, his mooring post. Thus, the bond the child forms is not with the person who elicited attachment; instead, this bond serves to make him capable of attachment, it enables him to enter into relationships. This anchorage opens up the world. Indeed, this process illustrates the paradox of any transferential moment or movement, and any encounter: a point of contact which does not lock two beings in a relation, but separates them and opens to the world. The encounter is always paradoxical, sustained by a connection-disconnection impulse. Beyond the encounter, there is the relation, where attachments are formed.

How does an "*I*" insert his particular tonality into the great collective human concert? How is one's place acquired? In a movement of connection-disconnection: connection through language, which marks directly in a constructive or destructive manner, depending on the reception given to the newborn, and on the words spoken at his birth; and disconnection, because the child takes possession of language and becomes the subject of his speech, the one who determines the relationship to be built with the environment in order to obtain what he needs for his life. Tying and untying are indissociable, set off against each other in a unifying, nominative process.

Thus, although in the session we display a mother's capacity for transformation, the child doesn't take us for his mother, or any mother in general. For him, there is never any confusion. He uses what we give him access to, for his life, like an adult does in an analysis. The space of availability we offer him encourages the advent of an encounter between two particular people, bringing two subjects, two living beings, into existence. In this space, we recognise the infant's full-fledged membership in the *Human Race*[15] by addressing him as a human being in his own right. He, in turn, confirms this status at the same time and just as spontaneously.

We have seen that the space of availability offered the infant cannot be an isolated bubble, since it is already inhabited by people in the baby's world – people belonging to the three sectors entrusted with their care by society – on whom the parents themselves rely. Thus, a chain of transference is set in place. This means that what is felt and what is said are compatible and are guided by a shared code of ethics.

Notes

1 Heidegger, M., *On the Way to Language*, Harperone, 1982.
2 Formulation used by psychoanalyst Lucien Kokh.
3 Freud, S., *The Complete Letters of Sigmund Freud to Wilhelm Fliess, 1887-1904*, Belknap Press, 1986. Letter dated Dec. 6, 1896, pp. 207–214.
4 Piera Aulagnier's concept.
5 Winnicott's concept of "object-presenting". In his view, the good-enough mother is one who presents the breast or bottle just when the baby needs it, giving him the illusion that he creates it and that it is his; she gives the baby the essential illusion that the breast is part of him. This space of illusion is where the child develops his ability to play and to create. Winnicott speaks here of the "found/created object".
6 Réfabert, P., *From Freud to Kafka*, Routledge, 2014, p. 6.
7 Winnicott's term.
8 Dolto, F., *Dominique: Analysis of an Adolescent*, Souvenir Press, 1974.
9 Name given by Winnicott to this function, the foundation of the maternal position. The mother's suitable care supports the child, contains and protects him. She acts as a "protective shield" against existential anxiety.
10 Is there a parallel between this ability to maintain all the languages in harmonious resonance, the foundation of the maternal function, and the resonance of the breath, the traditional idea of Qi (vital force) in Chinese medicine? Jacques Giès writes: "*Qi,* the breath, is associated with *yun,* resonance, to form *qiyun,* resonance of the breath" in the 2004 exhibition brochure, *Mountains and Waters. Celestial mountains. Treasures of the Museums of China* organised by Chinese national museums. Jacques Giès, curator at the *Guimet National Museum,* was a specialist in Buddhist painting from China and Central Asia.
11 Film, Byambasuren Davaa and Luigi Faloeni (Dirs.), Germany, 2003.
12 François Jullien coined the French term "relationner", meaning to bring attachment into being, to originate it.
13 Zaltzman, N., *De la guérison psychanalytique*, PUF, 1999. *The Human Race* is the title of a book by Robert Antelme.
14 Film, Carlos Saldanha (Dir.), 2009.
15 Antelme, R., *The Human Race*, Marlboro Press, 1998.

Chapter 4

Transference with Little Humans

In my psychoanalytic practice, over the course of 25 years, I saw not only adults, but also babies, accompanied by spokespersons: either their parents or trustworthy third parties, when the children were wards of Child Welfare Services (ASE in France).

Anxiety

For 25 years I was filled with anxiety before each session with an infant. The fear that precedes action, the dread before taking a leap, the void before the encounter. A subliminal acute perception of the absence of thought, necessary for entering the stage. Nudity. Dread at the thought of having to plunge into this obscure region of "primary maternal preoccupation". Will I be able to descend to the bottom of the well... and come back up within the short space of a session? François Roustang points out that this is a moment of "heightened vigilance",[1] of extreme concentration. We shall return to this question later, in our discussion of forgetting.

Zhuang-Zhou's words come to mind: "Emptying the mind allows energy to emerge. Emptiness is the means for efficacious action". Emptiness–fullness. Being empty of thought, of ego, in the presence of the subject's sensory fullness, his "feeling soul".[2]

This fearsome moment is experienced by the musician before a concert, by the painter who suspends his gesture in mid-air, the

DOI: 10.4324/9781003672791-4

actor about to enter the stage, the lover before his rendezvous, the psychoanalyst about to do his work. All of them acknowledge this experience. The French singer Barbara expressed it most vividly:

> I feel the audience arriving, I creep along stealthily behind the curtain, I breathe through this heavy, velvet curtain. This moment of entering the stage is extremely surprising […]. I am under the spell of the spectators assembled in the theatre hall. It's a state of hypnosis. I have the impression that if someone plunged a knife into my back while I am on the stage, I would not feel it.[3]

This moment is necessary to ignite creation, to solicit the emergence of the vital. "An unexpected encounter – the path emerges through the words attempting to be heard", as Lou, a Chinese psychotherapist, told me.

Will I be able to do justice to the beauty of the human race, to keep the promise of the dawn of life, to contribute to its accomplishment? I have observed that a baby in distress has incredible resources and courage, as well as the determination to be heard and obtain what he needs, provided he finds himself in an attentive and supportive environment. As soon as he feels that he is on solid ground, on a rock, he holds on tightly, as all living things do, from plants to humans.

The trust placed in me was crucial. Every human being strives to find his place. I walked in the footsteps of Françoise Dolto, who ushered in this faith in psychoanalysis for babies. I acquired this faith through what I would call "professional" transference. I had to take my place. I was surprised, destabilised, subjected to discomfort and irritation, anxiety and dismay. My desire to be good – in all senses of the word – contributed to this. I felt helpless, but I held on to what I considered solid: at first, to Dolto's faith and her convictions; later, to my own perceptions and feelings, to what I sensed, to my unconscious. I placed my trust in the babies, who were not giving up on their humanity.

The scenes the little ones play out, their "freeze frames" kept in suspense, had been awaiting an other who could be addressed, who could dispel their malediction, whose sensitive and lucid presence would transform these scenes into speech, put them into words, and cause the developmental process to resume where it left off.

Letting the infant express himself means placing oneself at risk. For indeed, he will express himself, and loudly! Life is a noisy affair.

Pleasure

But let us go back to Freud, to his *Project*,[4] where he speaks of an "experience of satisfaction", something particularly crucial for analysts who work with babies.

> When the extraneous helper has carried out the specific action [...] on behalf of the helpless subject, the latter is in a position, by means of reflex contrivances, immediately to perform what is necessary in the interior of his body in order to remove the endogenous stimulus. This total event then constitutes an "experience of satisfaction".[5]

There can be no better way to describe what happens every time we are able to perform the specific action required by the helpless person, whether it be the baby present before us, or the baby present in the adult in analysis. This specific action is an act of thought. To think is an action. And satisfaction is a bonus for both protagonists in the exchange.

In this text, Freud underscores the importance of pleasure in the economy of the psyche. In the consultation with a baby, satisfaction is the operative word. The pleasure taken in being together in the exchange, this affective and symbolic support – a veritable magic carpet – the underpinning of any encounter and openness to the other, is what allows the baby to express his pain, his rage, his distress.

Forgetting

The psychical work I had to do to be of help to these babies consisted mainly of pushing away the black or grey clouds floating above them, in the form of clusters of words said about them, accounts of their history, statements full of anguish describing dramas. I had to put words and speeches full of pity out of my mind, to be in a physical and psychical state that made me receptive to the living being, his enigma, his mystery, his beauty. For this reason, I had to *forget*. I had to forget, at least for the moment, in the immediacy of the encounter, the story told about this baby by adults, so that I could be present for the child who was there, in a state of *availability*. I believe this is what Freud is saying in the *Project*: that perceptions take shape in the neurons, that consciousness is connected to perceptions, although no trace of this event is left in the neurons because *memory and consciousness are mutually exclusive*. I was able to confirm this in my clinical practice: that presence – hence perception – and memory exclude each other.

This brings to mind the requirement of anonymity, a founding principle of the *Maison Verte*, a principle established by Marie-Hélène Malandrin and still in effect today. The other requirement at a *maison verte* is the physical presence of a parent or a designated substitute. In my consulting room, there were two inversely corresponding requirements: that of forgetting (for the duration of the session) the history, all the scrupulously gathered information – which I equate with the principle of anonymity – and the internalised presence in the analyst of the child's parents, who are not physically present.

Freud used the term "free-floating attention" to designate this disposition to *availability* needed by the analyst.

In a conference given in May 2017, Brazilian psychoanalyst Denise Maurano spoke of this attention in the following terms: "To arrive at a time of creation" (which is the essence of our work),

> the primordial time, the poet must drink from the Fountain of Lethe, from the spring of forgetting. This puts him in a precarious position. By inducing the forgetting of present quarrels, Mnemosyne makes it possible to access the time of origins.
>
> In an analysis, to let oneself be carried away by the flow of words, or to let words sing inside us, to let them resonate beyond the reach of speech structured by consciousness, we must allow ourselves to drink from the Fountain of Lethe. This is why, in order for what is essential to emerge, there must be a time of going adrift, as indispensable to the analysand as it is to the analyst. The attention must float on the waters of forgetting. This free-floating attention carries us to the regions of origins.

When I think back on the years doing this work, I would say that I practiced the equivalent of a spiritual activity. Before each session, I cast the dice. Would I be able to be there, present, was I ready for what could be a stroke of lightning, a *moment of transcendence, of spirituality, of grace*?

I can suppose that my impetus, the source of my creative energy, was located in a part of me that could only be reached in the presence of a "baby other". That part was the baby I had been, who was given a poor reception at birth, who was treated roughly and whose needs were ignored, a baby who barely escaped dying, as a doctor predicted, at the age of 18 months from bronchial pneumonia. I was saved by a more modern doctor who prescribed penicillin, the miracle drug made available after the war. But that baby's experience had been devoid of any reassuring words for her or her family. The poor reception, the rough treatment and the absence of words was very likely what led me to become a psychoanalyst later.

I strove, no doubt, to find these words over and over with each baby I encountered in my work, who brought with him the distress caused by the thwarting, attacking and breaking of his vital life impulse.

Listening to Babies Requires A Philosophical Attitude

Young parents know very well that the arrival of a baby turns everything upside down and ushers in the unexpected, so that they are no longer on solid ground. They face the frightening abyss of the unknown. The foundations are shaky, everything has to be rebuilt: the self, one's relation with the other and with all others. If the ground is disintegrating, everything could collapse. The encounter with this bundle of energy that a newborn is requires one to be sufficiently alive, in motion, flexible, adaptable. Françoise Dolto insisted that she had learned everything from babies. One of Gérard Guillerault's books dedicated to her is entitled *L'image du corps selon Françoise Dolto. Une philosophie clinique.*[6] Indeed, we engage in a philosophical practice. Working with babies forces us to be philosophical practitioners, to philosophise like children do. What does it mean to be a human being? What does it mean to encounter a little human being in therapy? Like all extreme situations, this work requires specific skill. I was guided in my practice by Nathalie Zaltzman's writing, particularly her book *De la guérison psychanalytique.*[7]

To undertake this work, we must rediscover the language of the body, a graphic language, our first maternal tongue, before the one that would become the maternal tongue we would speak.

In the course of my practice with babies, my thinking took place in my entire body. I am certain that this capacity for activation, for making an appeal and sending a message, which activates our own corresponding capacity to be a message for the other, exists since conception.

I believe it is what Lacan referred to when he wrote: "A signifier represents a subject for another signifier. That is, the subject does not represent himself to another subject directly" (Seminar XX).[8] This ability is at work in transference, of course, and in every form of creation, which may be seen as a projection of it on a two or three-dimensional support (painting or sculpture, for instance). This capacity lends its poetic spirit to all human creation, be it the mere fragment of a statue or a poem, as Peter Sloterdijk points out in the following passage on *the fragment and its ability to act as a message.*

Speaking of Rilke's poem "Archaic Torso of Apollo", he writes:

> It is reasonable to suppose that this work was also an expression of thanks to Rodin, his master in his Paris days, for the concept of the autonomous torso, which he had encountered in his workshop. The reason for the existence of the perfection conjured up in these fourteen lines is that it possesses – independently of its material carrier's mutilation – the authorization to form a message that appeals from within itself. This power of appeal is exquisitely evident in the object evoked here. The perfect thing is that which articulates an entire principle of living. The poem has to perform no more and no less than to perceive the principle of being in the thing and adapt it to its own existence – with the aim of becoming a construct with an equal power to convey a message.[9]

Notes

1 Roustang, F., *What Is Hypnosis?* Versilio, 2019.
2 Anthony, L., *Qu'est-ce que l'hypnose de François Roustang,* Flammarion/Versilio, 2019, p. 44.

3 Interview September 3, 1965. Exhibition Paris Philharmonic, October 13, 2017 – January 28, 2018.

4 I am grateful to Françoise Mona Besson for reminding me of this during the presentation of my book *Accomplir la promesse de l'aube* in the fall of 2017 at the *Ateliers de psychanalyse.*

5 Freud, S., *Project for a Scientific Psychology*, S.E. 1, London: Hogarth, p. 397.

6 Guillerault, G., *L'image du corps selon Françoise Dolto. Une philosophie clinique*, L'Institut Synthélabo, 1999.

7 Zaltzman, N., *De la guérison psychanalytique*, PUF, 1999.

8 Lacan, J., *The Seminar of Jacques Lacan. Book XVIII. On a Discourse that Might Not Be a Semblance*, Polity, 2025.

9 Sloterdijk, P., *You Must Change Your Life*, Hoban, W. (Trans.), Polity, 2014, p. 21.

Chapter 5

On Availability and Transference

Parents transmit life, they are go-betweens. The child emerges from an undifferentiated background, as Freud wrote in 1940, in *An Outline of Psycho-Analysis*:

> We may picture an initial state of things by supposing that the whole available energy of Eros, which we shall henceforth call "libido", is present in the Ego-Id, which has not yet been differentiated, and serves to neutralize the destructive tendencies that are present at the same time. [...] Everything that we know is related to the Ego, in which the entire available amount of libido is originally stored. We call this state absolute primary *narcissism*.[1]

In his short paper *The Antithetical Meaning of Primal Words*,[2] Freud comments on Carl Abel's pamphlet,[3] to discuss the relation between primitive languages and dream-work, in which contraries are disregarded and negation seems not to exist, and which represents "contraries as one and the same thing. We obtain [from Abel's study] the astonishing information that the behaviour of the dream-work which I have just described is identical with a peculiarity in the oldest languages known to us".[4]

Abel's object of study is the Egyptian language, but he also mentions Chinese (whose origins are ancient, while the

DOI: 10.4324/9781003672791-5

language itself is modern because it is spoken today). Contrary meanings of a word exist originally and disappear as the language evolves. Freud concludes: "And we psychiatrists cannot escape the suspicion that we should be better at understanding and translating the language of dreams if we know more about the development of language". Freud turns to the wisdom of Chinese Daoism, to the concept of a spontaneous invariable process regulating all things, which have equal value and are part of the same whole. Here, the original emotion is unspecific, without valence.

Distortions of language which inscribe the child in a false filiation – a denied and obliterated filiation, or distorted language which does not perform the function of welcoming the child into the world, can hinder the process. The parents' traumas can cause them to block the flow of vital energy in their children, to create deviations. We therapists are also go-betweens who step in to facilitate the unblocking of the babies' vital energy. We shall look more closely at these moments when, from an available space created in me, springs a word which brings into existence two living, desiring subjects. What disposition must I be in for this to happen? François Jullien answers: "To the Chinese, 'knowing' means not so much forming an idea about something, as making oneself available to [something]. Emptiness-calm-serenity-detachment: this disposition to availability is created by rejecting any specific disposition, limited and rigid (of the 'ego')".[5]

On Availability and Transference
How to Set Aside the Ego

"Leaning On His Armrest, Gazing Into space, Nan-kung K'uo was slowly emptying himself of his breath; he felt as if he had lost his body. Afterwards, King-ye Ch'ang, his

servant, who stood before him [...] asked: 'I have often seen
you leaning on your armrest, but never like this?'
   — You are right to ask, Nan-kung K'uo answered. Did
you notice that I lost my inner nature just then?"
                    Jean-François Billeter, *Études sur Tchang-tseu.*[6]

What is the state needed to allow listening that calls forth the
free and spontaneous flow of speech?

After the publication of *Studies on Hysteria* in 1895, Freud
abandoned hypnosis and invented the psychoanalytic tech-
nique. He formulated what was to be the fundamental rule for
analysts: "free-floating attention", *die frei/gleichschwebende
Aufmerksamkeit*, literally, "evenly suspended attention". In
response, "free association" was required of the analysand.
But is it enough for the analyst-analysand tandem to respect a
rule, to follow instructions? What is this particular state of consciousness needed for psychoanalysis, this suspension of will,
of knowledge, of judgement, of intention? This strategic stance
is doubly important because it also determines the stance of the
patient. How does the analyst reach this state? How does he
learn it? How does he cultivate it? To consider this question,
let us look at China, through the eyes of François Roustang,
François Jullien and Jean-François Billeter.

François Roustang, psychoanalyst and hypnotherapist,
explains the concept of "disposition", on which his practice of
hypnosis is founded:

It is a matter of how to awaken and keep awake generalised
vigilance [...] through a disposition, by disposing ourselves
to generalised wakefulness. This takes thought, of course,
but thought which acts, thought put into practice. This action
creates a different way of hearing, of seeing, of feeling [...].
In order to hear, see or feel in another way, we must, first
of all, not hear, see or feel. We must hear nothing, but let
things resonate; see nothing, but let the light be reflected;

feel nothing, but let what each of the senses perceives blend together. [...] Then, the one who hears will no longer be an external observer, he will be encompassed in these movements, he will take part in them, share, participate.[7]

Roustang warns:

It would be easy to object, to say that any psychoanalyst, psychotherapist or physician who takes his work seriously understands this disposition. As does any man or woman who does not take their interlocutor for a geometry theory. [...] we suppose that it is taken into account, or considered obvious, so that there is no need for it to become a specific object of study. There are also those who don't give disposition any thought.

In the chapter entitled "How Is Disposition Learned?", Roustang points out that disposition is not acquired once and for all. It resembles a plant that needs constant care in order to grow. We must come back to it over and over to bring it into existence again and again, to strengthen it and detect its weaknesses.
François Jullien tells us:

Potential stems from disposition.[8] This *acquisition through detachment* no longer focuses on an object; it *does not project*. It casts no shadow, is not guided by intentionality, and therefore grants equal importance to all things. Disposition creates a wide opening because it has no expectation.[9]

He maintains that Freud, being an Occidental man, was lacking a concept that would have allowed him to formulate this idea otherwise than in the negative: "Free-floating attention" is "diffuse attention, *not* focalised, *not* ruled by any intentionality".[10]
By contrast, in China the perspective is strategic rather than theoretical, oriented towards efficacy. "Availability" makes it

conceivable to "give all possibilities their chance". "*Knowledge*, without a specific direction, becomes *wakefulness* not suscep- tible to being reduced to a particular claim."[11] Availability is precisely the requirement for any cognitive process. I would not hesitate to resume the teaching of Chinese philosophy by say- ing: "The sage is he who has attained availability".[12]

In France, psychoanalysts are presumed to practice avail- ability. But how have they attained it? Their training is long and expensive. They must undertake a personal analysis (or more than one), which is no longer called "training" analysis, but rather "therapeutic analysis" of which they may be asked to give an account before their peers. When making the tran- sition from analysand to analyst, the latter is given guidance. His supervisor listens and supports him in his work. The ana- lyst continues his training by regular reading of psychoanalytic texts alone or in a work group, by attending study days, confer- ences and discussions with other clinicians.

The experience of an analysand and that of an analyst cannot be superposed. This particular listening, this state of availability requiring the suspension of intentionality, emptying the mind to create an active void where thoughts will come together – this listening depends on a discipline of body and mind.

> To arrive at this, counting on reason alone does not suffice, but we can't depend on a state of grace either. What is needed is a discipline of the mind, which is (first of all) a discipline of the body: the breath, breathing.[13]

How do transmission and learning take place? What possible paths can one take to train oneself to practice this form of free- floating attention which requires "great vigilance" and makes the unconscious available? These questions were of interest to Wilfred Bion, a British analyst born in India, and a contem- porary of Jacques Lacan. Bion's work focused closely on clin- ical experience. In France, these questions have not really been

examined. But the practice of psychoanalysis offers both analyst and analysand the opportunity to innovate.

Detours are possible, incursions into other spheres: music,
painting, literature, as well as the human sciences, life sciences
and hard sciences such as quantum physics. The list is not
exhaustive. Changing perspectives, changing languages, translating... are all detours giving access to availability. "Travelling
without papers, crossing borders freely from one field of knowledge to another", as Abram de Swaan[14] says, lets a new way of
thinking emerge, thinking that is alive, free, unrestrained.

Nothing in our Western culture has prepared us for a state
of availability – on the contrary. Freud's heirs are suspicious
of anything that might seem unscientific. Freud needed to be
recognised and respected by his peers while he was founding
a new science. Theories about psychic processes, themselves
distinct objects of study in the continuity of Cartesian solipsism
and the division operated by science, examined the subject and
his objects. They described the human, whose specificity is the
ability to speak, as part of a world of objects, not an interactive
world. For a long time, these theories did not attempt to shed
light on the more shadowy area of the *in-between*, between subjects, between a subject and the world, between worlds. They
failed to consider the continuity between the human and the
world, a question of great interest to Chinese philosophy.

We must become familiar with both approaches – the
Occidental and the Oriental. Many contemporary writers have
undertaken this work. For instance, in his book *Eyes*, Michel
Serres elaborates on his intuition that the world looks at us.[15] He
wishes there could be a "Museum of Seeing", more precisely
of seeing and being seen, where we could see with the eyes of
stones, of animals, of the sea, of letters. Physicist Carlo Rovelli
asserts:

There is nothing in our makeup that eludes nature's regularities. If something in us ran counter to these regularities, we

would have discovered it long ago. Nothing in us violates the natural behaviour of things. All of modern science, from physics to chemistry, from biology to the neurosciences, has done nothing but reinforce this observation.[16]

European man has lost his position as the centre of the world; man has yet to lose his position as the centre of the universe. But he has much to gain by becoming a living being among others – his survival at the very least.

Our culture has not prepared us for a state of availability, although... every psychoanalyst knows that if an analysis produces a change in the patient's life, it is not thanks to any theories. The effect is produced by an element of surprise, by the unexpected emergence of something neither the analyst nor the analysand suspected, in a moment of encounter between their unconscious worlds, or, more accurately, between the two people at a level unknown to them – something of which they may become aware in the aftermath. When the thought is formulated, the event has already taken place. Something has happened. The aim is to facilitate the encounter, not to connect two egos. For this to happen, the ego must not silence the "I".

The contributions of contemporary science, particularly the neurosciences, have validated our scientific discoveries. They have provided us with images of what we observe in our practice. These images of the brain confirm the largely unconscious nature of its activity. For instance, it has been confirmed that babies *really* understand language: it is now indisputable that human beings have a biological predisposition to speech. Two or three amino acids we possess, while chimpanzees do not, are responsible for this, according to Anne Christophe, CNRS[17] researcher and director of the psycholinguistic laboratory of the Port-Royal Hospital in Paris. Jacques Pelegrin, research director at the CNRS, explains that when he carved flint, *Homo erectus* was already engaged in narrating. Carving a double-sided object and constructing a sentence activate the same cerebral region: the parietal lobe. The carving of flint blades presupposes the ability to organise, to describe the world; this activity is as complex as a game of chess. At the dawn of human history, just like at the dawn of life of a little human, everything is already present, encoded.

Discoveries about the brain, about its right and left hemispheres, encourage us to conceive of and develop a different way of educating the thinking process, which would make more room for the emotional element. We think with our bodies, our emotions, our imagination; we think thanks to a state of availability to the world. Thought springs forth from this state, which can be learned just as we learned to read and write, with the help of a method. This must become a discipline for everyday living.

In the 4th century BC, Zhuang Zhou used imaginary dialogues to talk about the existence of "activity systems". One of these is a system where activity is "effective", "spontaneous" and "necessary", "complete" or "whole" in that it results from the conjunction of "all faculties and resources we possess".[18] The activity system superior to this one seems to correspond to what we call the "unconscious".

In *Études sur Tchouang-tseu*,[19] Jean-François Billeter translates a dialogue imagined by Zhuang Zhou between Confucius and Lao Tzu, dialogue XV.[20] Here, Zhuang Zhou speaks of the state of undifferentiated receptivity needed for a transformation to take place. Billeter comments:

> One cannot expect to produce a transformation in someone else unless he accepts to be transformed himself. This law seems to me to apply to all forms of human interaction, from the most basic to the most complex, from the most intuitive to the most cerebral.[21]

Quite possibly, this concise formulation conveys the secret of the effectiveness of the analytic situation. In his straightforward definition of effective speech which is an act, and which can only emerge from a specific internal state, Billeter compares Saint Paul's position to that of Zhuang Zhou (pointing out that the latter had no need of God): "They both recognised this fundamental paradox, that freedom is produced and produces us".[22]

"Do not listen with your ears, but with your mind. Do not listen with your mind, but with your energy. [...] energy is a completely receptive void. The act is accomplished only in this void."[23] To listen with one's energy requires being present in one's own body while perceiving the other's life energy. It seems to me that this is how the work with babies is accomplished. The act referred to in this imaginary dialogue is spontaneous speech. The emphasis is on the place from which spontaneous speech emerges: "I call the place where no thing encounters its opposite, the shift in the way. The speech emerging from this place is not a discursive answer to a previous discourse, but rather an act which transforms a situation".[24] Zhuang Zhou identifies the state resulting from the cessation of all intentionality, that is, "visionary" knowledge, from which "great speech" emerges.[25]

It could be supposed that these texts inspired Jacques Lacan to define interpretation as "full speech", as opposed to "empty speech", and as a way of insisting on a necessary loss of *ego* on the part of the analyst: setting the ego aside to let the subject of the unconscious speak. In Seminar XVIII, Lacan comments that studying Chinese in his youth with his teacher Paul Démiéville played a crucial role in what he would become: "I have noticed [...] that perhaps I am Lacanian because I formerly studied Chinese".[26]

Lacan's formulations provide me with words to describe my experience as it relates to the moment of divestment. In anticipation of it, I feared it, I felt like the tightrope walker before he starts his walk above the abyss. Most of the time, I "forgot" what I had been told about the child, his family, his history (although these things existed somewhere in my being). I was completely disarmed, naked, as I faced the baby and his body which spoke in sign language, sending messages.

But what I am sure of is that the baby is saved solely by clinging to life. Psychoanalysts speak of a "desiring subject", while Chinese philosophers speak simply of a self with its energy. Divestment is followed by emergence: the emergence of speech that always clashes with a devastating ambiance, a tragic narrative – speech which creates a space, which drives back the dramatic events in order to welcome the living child.

Looking back at my patients, the reader will remember Laura, who was thought of as a body, as wounded buttocks. When I spoke to her of her rejected femininity, she answered at once: "Look". Let both of us girls admire the garden (a feminine symbol) side by side. And Fred, who became animated when I remarked on his "appetite for joy" rather than milk. As well as Samira, who was enlivened by my confirmation of her right to sleep, simply because she, like all infants, needs to sleep.

In the sessions, when my positioning is in resonance with the babies' potential life energy, an immediate transformative effect is produced, on them and on me. I then have a comforting feeling of plenitude, born of the gratification created by the fleeting certainty of being a human being equal to another human being.

Contemporary authors have introduced me to philosophers of Ancient China whose formulations have helped me to reflect on what I call, in a line of thought passed down by Sigmund Freud and Jacques Lacan, transference, the cornerstone of psychoanalytic practice. This particular state of consciousness or unconsciousness is of primordial importance when working with babies – while with adults, the not-knowing and not-desiring state also constitutes the basis of the encounter, but is diverted by the use of speech.

In the void, words are thrown out like the pebbles strewn by Little Thumbling; they draw a line between the interlocutors. Many twists and turns will be needed before discovering, in a sudden flash, what the baby is experiencing.

This "receptive disposition" characterises a person who can set himself aside in the encounter with the other. That is, he loses his *ego* in favour of the *I* which goes towards the other, thus allowing this other *I* to exist. This receptivity requires a paradoxical ability: forgetting one's *ego* and accepting the position of unconscious subject.

On Transference and Transformation

> *"Expectation Colored By hope and faith is an effective force with which we have to reckon [...] in all our attempts at treatment and cure."*
> Sigmund Freud, *Findings, Ideas, Problems.*[27]

> *"There is a particular transference of the analyst, who believes in this human being, his interlocutor, a unique being, subject of the symbolic function, a subject wishing to signify himself, a subject seeking an answer to his question."*
> Françoise Dolto, *Dominique: Analysis of an Adolescent.*[28]

These statements place us at the foundations, in the sphere of faith, of belief. The Latin etymology of the word "confidence" is composed of *cum*, "with" and *fidere* "to have faith, to trust". To trust together. Confidence is what is woven *between* two people, based on faith. The Robert dictionary defines faith as the assurance given to be true to one's word, to do as one says. Alain Rey's *Dictionnaire culturel* (Cultural Dictionary) adds some essential details:

> In Latin: *fides*, in the subjective sense, is rooted in a relation between the individual and the word – truthful word or promise – considered worthy or unworthy of trust. [...] by equating *credo*, "I believe", as well as "I trust" (in God) with *fides*, the word designating this belief, the Latin of Christianity incorporates "faith" into religion, its religion...

The legal, linguistic and logical [...] as well as ethical and psychological perspectives [...] are therefore absorbed in the tending towards the revealed God.[29]

Thus, the religious meaning is secondary.

This question of confidence is present in the texts of Chinese philosophers who cannot be suspected of mysticism. Friendship is based on lengthy acquaintance, which produces it and makes it last. Similarly, in the business world, it is not with strangers that contracts are signed. *Accomplish, promise, loyal, word*: these are terms found in the human as well as the psychoanalytic contract. Today, in everyday language and in the human sciences, words like *soul, faith, joy, humility, goodness*, for example, are considered suspect due to their religious connotation. But without them, how can we speak of the human condition?

As we just mentioned, Freud defined transference as a "dynamic force" generated by "expectation colored by hope and faith". Françoise Dolto spoke of transference "specific to the analyst" who "believes in the human being". As for the etymological definition of "transference", the Robert dictionary reads:

> *Transference*: the action of transferring. *Trans*: movement beyond, passage from one place to another
> *Ferro*: to carry, to have in oneself or in one's possession. To take towards, to give. To put forth, to push forward. To lead. To conduct. To take away. To destroy. To carry away, to receive, to bear, to be subjected to, to request, to want, to give birth to, bring into existence, to manifest, to narrate, to propose. To inscribe in a register.

... The transference activates all these meanings.

Psychoanalysts have encountered difficulties in the handling of this essential tool: the transference. One error is the idea that the analyst has only to be there to receive the subject's solicitation, for the work to be accomplished. Staying silent is not enough. To presume that the patient can do the work alone is, in fact, to repeat the crime. Indeed, what has caused the greatest suffering to patients was having been left to themselves (which does not mean that they were alone). No, the response to a subject's solicitation must be the *address to him made by another*.

Another error is the idea that the transference must be explained; it is presumed that the patient's suffering and blockages will be abolished by these explanations. But this is not so. Talking about the transference has no effect. In truth, the work is done together, the experience is shared by two people. In the transference, each person holds up the other.

The space where the transference takes place is the very site of the metaphor, the space of immediate-mediated speech. The Greek root of metaphor means, literally, "transport, moving" (in Greece, one can read this word on the side of moving trucks). Transference and metaphor are closely linked: "In its functioning, the metaphor is an instant mediation; this is what makes it exemplary: it *suddenly* brings forth what it carries over to the other. It gives immediate access to it while carrying it across".[30]

In the session with very young children, there is immediate transport, transference to another – the analyst, who has ancestral, immemorial knowledge. No matter how young the child is, a connection is established between the singular and the world, at the place where *transference* occurs, at the site of the metaphor. Transference is a metaphorical situation giving access to *living*, accomplishing the promise of life.

Let us look back at the clinical work. When I welcome John and share his emotion with him, I am the spokesperson, the representative of the parents of his prehistory. To quote Freud:

> The effects of the first identifications made in earliest childhood will be general and lasting. This leads us back to the

origin of the ego ideal; for behind it there lies hidden an individual's first and most important identification; his identification with the father (with the parents) in his own personal
prehistory. This is apparently not in the first instance the
consequence or outcome of an object-cathexis; it is a direct
and immediate identification and takes place earlier than any
object-cathexis.[31]

When Samira opens her eyes under my gaze, which she has
solicited, she acts out a birth scene where the baby opens her
eyes and sees for the first time a world where someone is happy
to welcome her. She appealed to me to playact-live, with her, a
happy, dignified, humanised arrival into the world.

As for Yannis, he playacts over and over his emergence from
the uterus, from the tight enclosure. I remember how he pulled
his foot away when he touched the ground, like a child would
do if he touched a hot surface. We now know about the burning
sensation felt in nerve endings as a result of deprivation. As a
witness, I feel the torment in my own body; and just as happens
when a mother can calm her child by bearing his pain, when she
can finally put it into words appeasement follows.

Fatou invites me to witness the scene of the bottle feeding.
When I understand (stand under) her dread and distress, she is
pacified and my own tension dissolves. Just as is done on the
set of a movie, we repeat the scene until it is played just right.

In the session with Yannis and his mother, I am rendered
speechless by the slap on the baby's hand when he wants to
draw, to express himself. Without knowing it, I am asked to
think, for both of us, about the effects of violence on a baby's
instinct development.

In these situations, I am trans-posed, carried across to another
scene, summoned personally to a scene in my own history, with
my ability to think it through, which will serve both of us. We
accompany each other in this return to the origins. My verbal
and non-verbal interventions are, most often, displacements,

detours, sidesteps creating a space where the babies can start to breathe. To formulate a thought is, in itself, to make a detour.

Notes

1 Freud, S., *An Outline of Psycho-Analysis*, S.E. 23, London: Hogarth, p. 32.
2 Freud, S., *The Antithetical Meaning of Primal Words*, S.E. 11, London: Hogarth.
3 Abel, C., *The Antithetical Meaning of Primal Words*, Leipzig: Friedrich, 1884.
4 Freud, S., *The Antithetical Meaning of Primal Words*, S.E. 11, London: Hogarth, p. 161.
5 Jullien, F., *A Treatise on Efficacy: Between Western and Chinese Thinking*, Lloyd, J. (Trans.), University of Hawaii Press, 2004.
6 Billeter, J.-F., *Études sur Tchang-tseu*, Allia, 2004, p. 122.
7 Roustang, F., *What Is Hypnosis?* Versilio, 2019.
8 Jullien, F., *The Propensity of Things: Toward a History of Efficacy in China*, Zone Books, 1995.
9 Jullien, F., *Cinq concepts proposés à la psychanalyse*, Grasset, 2012.
10 Jullien, F., *Cinq concepts proposés à la psychanalyse*, Grasset, 2012.
11 Jullien, F., *Cinq concepts proposés à la psychanalyse*, Grasset, 2012.
12 Jullien, F., *Cinq concepts proposés à la psychanalyse*, Grasset, 2012., p. 36.
13 Jullien, F., *Cinq concepts proposés à la psychanalyse*, Grasset, 2012., pp. 202–203.
14 De Swaan, A., radio program France Culture, "La fabrique de l'histoire", Feb. 1, 2016.
15 Serres, M., *Eyes*, Bloomsbury Academic, 2015.
16 Rovelli, C., *Seven Brief Lessons on Physics*, Penguin, 2017.
17 National Centre for Scientific Research.
18 Billeter, J.-F., *Leçons sur Tchouang-tseu*, Allia, 2004, p. 46.
19 Billeter, J.-F., *Études sur Tchouang-tseu*, Allia, 2004, ch. II, "No Power, No Desire".
20 Billeter, J.-F., *Études sur Tchouang-tseu*, Allia, 2004, p. 64.
21 Billeter, J.-F., *Études sur Tchouang-tseu*, Allia, 2004, p. 66.
22 Billeter, J.-F., *Études sur Tchouang-tseu*, Allia, 2004, p. 113.

23 Billeter, J.-F., *Études sur Tchouang-tseu*, Allia, 2004, p. 80. Imaginary dialogue between Confucius and his disciple Yen Houei, verse 16.

24 Billeter, J.-F., *Études sur Tchouang-tseu*, Allia, 2004, p. 149.

25 Billeter, J.-F., *Études sur Tchouang-tseu*, Allia, 2004, ch. IV, "Cessation, Vision, Language".

26 Lacan, J., *The Seminar of Jacques Lacan. Book XVIII. On a Discourse that Might Not Be a Semblance*, Polity, 2025.

27 Freud, S., *Findings, Ideas, Problems*, S.E. 23, London: Hogarth, pp. 299–300.

28 Dolto, F., *Dominique: Analysis of an Adolescent,* Souvenir Press, 1974.

29 Rey, A., *Dictionnaire historique de la langue française*, Le Robert, 1992.

30 Jullien, F., *The Philosophy of Living*, Seagull Books, 2022.

31 Freud, S., *The Ego and the Id*, S.E. 19, London: Hogarth, p. 31.

Closing

The Chinese symbol above, which means "writing, letter, character", represents a little human under his roof, in his home; a baby who has to be pampered and protected, and who is taught by the written characters. This symbol refers to both the written trace and to the person who inscribes it, the one who must learn to hold a brush in order to be human.

Jacques Lacan described psychoanalysis as a "discipline that can survive only by maintaining itself at the level of an integral experience".

Let it be renounced, then, by whoever cannot rejoin at its horizon the subjectivity of his time. For how could he possibly make his being the axis of so many lives if he knew nothing of the dialectic that engages him with these lives in a symbolic movement? Let him be well acquainted with the whorl into which his period draws him in the continued enterprise of Babel, and let him be aware of his function as interpreter in the discord of languages.[2]

DOI: 10.4324/9781003672791-6

Figure 8

How, then, is it possible to continue *listening*? How can one go on doing this work without losing his ability to "spring forth",[3] how can one remain lively and creative?

The practice of psychoanalysis requires maintaining a gap, leaving a space for emergence, it requires practicing *distancing*. One must be able to maintain an *in-between* position and not become stuck. With adults, a day spent listening would put me in a meditative state, a state of altered consciousness. Working with traumatised babies has intensified this phenomenon since, with them, I could do nothing but let the signs conveyed by their bodies resonate within me. I discovered that what I took for a weakness in my thinking, my experiencing of a void, was in fact the key, the strategic lever of the mechanism. This happened *despite myself*, without *consent from my ego*. I regretted not having been prepared for it; had I been, I could have avoided unidentified suffering. This is one of the reasons for which I am trying to shed light on this phenomenon today.

My earlier description of the work done with a number of babies has no doubt made it clear what I mean by "the flow of life". Our work is to unblock this flow, by being in tune with it. These children are alive, we have only to let life do its work, while adopting an attitude free of intent and of knowing. Our role is to welcome life, to be in tune with it.

The babies I saw were exposed from birth, and some earlier, to maternal depression. My own experience, which agrees with that of other authors, confirms the essential role this plays in the development of a psychopathology of the *infans*. Piera Aulagnier writes:

> What characterises all depressive experience is that it destroys the "surplus of pleasure" which should result from action, thought, contact: the infant reacts to this absence, to this inability of the mother to express, to signal, to show in her contact with the child that she is alive and shares a pleasurable experience with him.[4]

Indeed, my ability to take pleasure in our encounters was what was needed in the work with the babies I described. Despite the tragic circumstances of their conception and birth, they awakened my capacity to marvel at life, at its emergence, and aroused my respect for their life energy potential, in resonance with mine.

Instead of "surplus of pleasure", I would rather say "principal" pleasure, the motor of the work, the element which makes it possible. This capacity for pleasure is directly related to my emotional need, my fascination with – we might even say my constantly renewed desire to contemplate – the mystery. The need to experience as a certainty the specificity of our humanity, which makes us equal, the need to experience these grace-filled moments.

A long time ago, when I started to work as an analyst, I had a dream. I was in a room, a large library. Outside, there was war, fire, destruction, persecutions. In the room, the walls were lined with books and, on the shelves, interspersed among the books, there were babies, naked newborns in foetal position.

To hold on to the pen, to the brush, to draw letters, characters; to hold on to life, grasp it firmly, follow its course. Babies, books – both are reminders of humanity's ancestral legacy.

In Chinese, writing and speech are differentiated from the start. Ideography is a form of writing which must be seen rather than heard to be understood. It was invented to record divinations, not discourses. Over time, it has been modified, but it has remained a written language separate from the spoken language. It could even serve as a paradigm of the relation between body language and the spoken word.

I remember my joy when I learned that the early ideogram for "writing, character, word" shows a newborn in the shelter of his home! The Chinese ideogram on the cover of this book was painted by Shu-Ling Lin. The same symbol opens this chapter. I continue to learn to read to decipher, to translate, to write: to be humanised.

I came to think of life as an energy-driven process by discovering the foundations of another culture and by working with these babies conceived and born in conditions which cancel any conventional discourse on love, desire and the couple. All those love stories we tell our children, knowing very well that they are fairy tales, fiction...

How, then, can we invent narratives, since a child must be able to construct a story of his origins, no matter what conditions he was born in? It is the anchorage point of his *id*. This work requirement also became a life practice, a spiritual practice that did away with many preconceived ideas.

I was led to step out of the conceptual framework of the Western world, and to look elsewhere – in China – for a conception of the origins closer to what the babies and I were experiencing. Life springs forth and develops where it pleases, disregarding any notion of desire, and everything occurring in human life must be humanised by being put into words.

Thanks to this practice with babies, I developed a receptivity that I hope was also useful to my other patients. Philippe Réfabert formulated this idea as follows: "Every crucial moment of human existence calls upon the transitional matrix that governs the passage from fetal life to breathing [...] from adolescence to adulthood".[5] And I would add: from working life to retirement, to old age, to death.

This capacity which develops in a relation between at least two people – the baby and the environment-mother – forms the basis of transference and the ability to change. Both sexes can develop this capacity.

Having this capacity changed my relation to time, since I was forced to live in the present moment, not to postpone, to be there, present at the right time. The urgency of certain situations and the anxiety they caused made this imperative. My relation to pleasure changed as well. These babies manifested the pleasure of being alive. The energy for pleasure is given along with life.

My relation to representation has changed. My ability to speak spontaneously, to use words that come from I know not where, to trust my unconscious, have all been reinforced. These children forced me to conceive of the unthinkable, to speak the unspeakable, to create representations of horror. They forced me to see that contrary factors exerted a combined effect, even without any attempt at reconciling them. Life-death. Horror-beauty. When I spoke to them, I found the words we needed in order not to be overwhelmed by evil, to deal with the dark side of life.

How should one accompany the anchoring of the life of a baby whose conception was barbaric? Or a baby who is an off-spring of incest? A baby whose only memory of his father is the odour of his corpse? A baby raped at 18 months? I am always outraged when I hear adults deny with great assurance that babies experience what happens to them. "No, no, they know nothing about it. Only their parents do." Denial does not help the baby inscribe the early traumatic events of his history; he simply "cuts them out". Aside from the fact that his immature psyche would not be able to assume them subjectively, they are cut out, or "split off" as is commonly said, because adults can't conceive of them for themselves, and much less for the child. The void in the child's psyche reflects the void in the adult's thinking. Therefore, I was being asked to think at this place of denial, the denial of evil, we might say.

Lastly, my view of the patients' complaints has changed. Many people who had been in analysis for years and who came to see me, were still trapped in their resentment towards their parents, and found it impossible to move forward, to create something living. Psychoanalytic discourse on the void, on lack, on pain and frustration, with its references to famous Greek myths, has fostered a culture of suffering, of complaint, of tragedy; it has ushered in well-being therapies and personal development therapies – now discredited by the same discourse.

Working with these babies makes it impossible to simply contemplate the horror. These babies are there, alive, with their immense potential, but frozen. They accustomed me to think of their parents, of their genitors, no matter how inadequate, with compassion. They reminded me of what is essential in our human condition. They placed life outside the sphere of tragedy, outside the conceptual sphere of happiness and misfortune. They led me to discover China where, since ancient times, the thinking excludes tragedy as a fundamental element of culture.

When I see in my office a little child crushed by the reality of his life, who can only send out "signs", pleas for help to whoever might hear, what I must do is pave the way for enchantment to enter this disenchanted childhood. I am there to affirm the magic of existence, of the possible – the necessary enchantment of life. My mission is to provide the child with means of access to it by making use of the treasures in my heart and in language, associated with my expertise. These children must know, from the beginning, that a human life is not determined by the madness of its origins.

What is needed is to construct the narratives most conducive to the development of the children's potential. Children have the closest possible relation to the power of words, they benefit from it fully. Little by little, this power is confiscated. It is with infants that we see it in full force. Of course, poets have never lost this power. Sometimes, parents have it. Sometimes, certain psychoanalysts.

This is what the work is about: keeping the *Promise at Dawn*.[6] In his short story "Ariadne", Chekhov wrote: "When I am nailed up in my coffin I believe I shall still dream of those early mornings, you know, when the [dawning] sun hurts your eyes …".[7]

I am not naïve enough to imagine that the lives of these children will be cloudless, but I like to think that the work we did together was an opportunity which gave them strength, and the certainty that it is possible to appeal to another and be heard.

If it happened once, it can happen again.

Notes

1 Gary, R., *Le sens de ma vie, Entretien*, Gallimard, 2014.
2 Lacan, J., "The Function and Field of Speech and Language", in *Écrits: A Selection*, Sheridan, A. (Trans.), London: Tavistock, 1977, p. 78.
3 Jullien, F., *Living Off Landscape*, Rodriguez, P. (Trans.), Rowman & Littlefield, 2018.
4 Aulagnier, P., & Dayan, M., *Un interprète en quête de sens*, Payot, 2016.
5 Réfabert, P., *From Freud to Kafka*, Routledge, 2014, p. 41.
6 Gary, R., *Promise at Dawn*, New Directions, 1987.
7 Chekhov, A., *Ariadne and Other Stories*, New York: Sovereign Publishing, 2012.

Bibliography

Abel, C., *The Antithetical Meaning of Primal Words*, Leipzig: Friedrich, 1884.

Antelme, R., *The Human Race*, Marlboro Press, 1998.

Anthony, L., *Qu'est-ce que l'hypnose de François Roustang*, Flammarion/Versilio, 2019

Arasse, D., *Take a Closer Look*, Waters, A. (Trans.), Princeton University Press, 2013.

Aulagnier, P., *The Violence of Interpretation*, London: Routledge, 2001.

Aulagnier, P., *Un interprète en quête de sens*, Payot, 2001.

Aulagnier, P., & Dayan, M., *Un interprète en quête de sens*, Payot, 2016.

Billeter, J.-F., *Études sur Tchouang-tseu*, Allia, 2004.

Billeter, J.-F., *Leçons sur Tchouang-tseu*, Allia, 2002.

Bion, W., *Learning from Experience*, Routledge, 1984.

Céline, L.-F., *Journey to the End of the Night*, New York: New Directions, 2006.

Chekhov, A., *Ariadne and Other Stories*, New York: Sovereign Publishing, 2012.

Crespin, G.C., *Traitement des troubles du spectre autistique*, érès, 2013.

Darrieussecq, M., *Il faut beaucoup aimer les hommes*, Gallimard, 2015.

Davoine, F., *Wittgenstein's Folly*, Routledge, 2023.

Davoine, F. & Gaudilière, J.-M., *History Beyond Trauma*, Other Press, 2004.

De Balzac, H., *The Lily of the Valley*, Waring, J. (Trans.), Philadelphia: The Gebbie Publishing Co., 1898.

De Bary, W.T., & Bloom, I. (Eds.), *Sources of Chinese Tradition*, Columbia University Press, 1999.

Des Forêts, L.-R., *Ostinato*, Cows, Mary Anne (Trans.), University of Nebraska Press, 2002.

Dolto, F., *Dominique: Analysis of an Adolescent*, Souvenir Press, 1974.

Dolto, F., *Le transfert dans le travail avec les enfants*, Schauder, C. (Ed.), érès, 2005.

Dolto, F., *L'image inconsciente du corps*, Seuil, 1984.

Dolto, F., *Lorsque l'enfant paraît*, Seuil, 1997.

Dolto, F., *Psychanalyse et pédiatrie*, Seuil, 1976.

Dolto, F., *Tout est langage*, Éditions de la Seine, 1987.

Faure, E., *History of Art IV*, Pack, W. (Trans.), New York and London: Harper & Brothers, 1924.

Freud, S., *An Outline of Psycho-Analysis*, S.E. 23, London: Hogarth.

Freud, S., *Findings, Ideas, Problems*, S.E. 23, London: Hogarth.

Freud, S., *New Introductory Lectures on Psycho-Analysis*, S.E. 22, London: Hogarth.

Freud, S., *Project for a Scientific Psychology*, S.E. 1, London: Hogarth.

Freud, S., *The Antithetical Meaning of Primal Words*, S.E. 11, London: Hogarth.

Freud, S., *The Complete Letters of Sigmund Freud to Wilhelm Fliess, 1887-1904*, Belknap Press, 1986.

Freud, S., *The Ego and the Id*, S.E. 19, London: Hogarth.

Freud, S., *The Origins of Psycho-Analysis: Letters to Wilhelm Fliess, Drafts and Notes, 1887–1902*, Kessinger Publishing, 2007.

Gary, R., *Le sens de ma vie, Entretien*, Gallimard, 2014.

Gary, R., *Promise at Dawn*, New Directions, 1987.

Giès, J., Hui, Y., & Riboud, P., *Les montagnes et les eaux, Trésors des musées de Chine*, Paris: Réunion des musées nationaux, 2004.

Golder, E.M., *Au seuil de la clinique infantile*, érès, 2013.

Green, A., "The Dead Mother", in *On Private Madness*, Routledge, 1996.

Guillerault, G., *L'image du corps selon Françoise Dolto. Une philosophie clinique*, L'Institut Synthélabo, 1999.

Harari, Y.N., *Sapiens: A Brief History of Humankind*, Harper, 2015.

Heidegger, M., *On the Way to Language*, Harperone, 1982.

Heraclitus, *Fragments*, Haxton, B. (Trans.), Penguin Classics, 2003.

Jablonka, I., *A History of the Grandparents I Never Had*, Stanford University Press, 2016.

Jullien, F., *A Treatise on Efficacy: Between Western and Chinese Thinking*, Lloyd, J. (Trans.), University of Hawaii Press, 2004.

Jullien, F., *Cinq concepts proposés à la psychanalyse*, Grasset, 2012

Jullien, F., *De l'intime, loin du bruyant amour*, Grasset, 2013.

Jullien, F., *In Praise of Blandness*, Zone Books, 2004.

Jullien, F., *L'écart et l'entre*, Galilée, 2012.

Jullien, F., *Living Off Landscape*, Rodriguez, P. (Trans.), Rowman & Littlefield, 2018.

Jullien, F., *The Philosophy of Living*, Seagull Books, 2022.

Jullien, F., *The Propensity of Things: Toward a History of Efficacy in China*, Zone Books, 1995.

Jullien, F., *Unexceptional Thought*, Rowman & Littlefield, 2020.

Lacan, J., "The Function and Field of Speech and Language", in *Écrits: A Selection*, Sheridan, A. (Trans.), London: Tavistock, 1977.

Lacan, J., *The Seminar of Jacques Lacan. Book XVIII. On a Discourse that Might Not Be a Semblance*, Polity, 2025.

Latrouite-Ma, M., "Yin and Yang, the Process of Separation in the Infant. A Chinese reading of a fort-da passage", *Le Coq-héron*, No. 237, 2019/2.

Lemaitre, P., *The Great Swindle*, Quercus, 2016.

Maspero, F., *Les abeilles et la guêpe*, Seuil, 2002.

Réfabert, P., *From Freud to Kafka*, Routledge, 2014.

Roustang, F., *What Is Hypnosis?* Versilio, 2019.

Rovelli, C., *Seven Brief Lessons in Physics*, Penguin, 2017.

Salvayre, L., *Pas pleurer*, Points, 2022.

Semprun, J., *The Long Voyage*, Seaver, R. (Trans.), New York: The Overlook Press, 2005.

Serres, M., *Eyes*, Bloomsbury Academic, 2015.

Sloterdijk, P., *You Must Change Your Life*, Hoban, W. (Trans.), Polity, 2014.

Strasbourg Conference 2004, *Françoise Dolto et le transfert, dans le travail avec les enfants*, érès, 2005.

Vincent, J.D., & Lledo, P.M., *The Custom-Made Brain: Cerebral Plasticity, Regeneration, and Enhancement*, Columbia University Press, 2014.

Virgil, *The Aeneid*, Book XI, Cambridge University Press, 2020.

Winnicott, D.W., *Playing and Reality*, Tavistock Publications, 1971.

Winnicott, D.W., *Talking to Parents*, Da Capo Lifelong Books, 1993.

Winnicott, D.W., *Through Pediatrics to Psychoanalysis*, New York: Basic Books, 1975.

Wittgenstein, L., *On Certainty*, Wiley Blackwell, 1991.

Zaltzman, N., *De la guérison psychanalytique*, PUF, 1999.

Index

Abel, Carl 94, 108, 118
anchorage 83, 114
ASE 19, 20, 24, 30, 32, 44, 86
attachment 27, 31, 82–85
Aulagnier, Piera 74, 77, 80, 85, 112, 117, 118
availability 3, 9, 22, 26, 84, 89, 94, 95, 97–99, 100, 101

Billeter, Jean-François 16, 18, 96, 101, 102, 108, 109
Bion, Wilfred 12, 37, 38, 79, 98, 118

child care assistants 7
Child Welfare Services x, 7, 86
Crespin, G. C. 17, 118

disposition 89, 95–97, 104
Dolto, Françoise 1, 3, 7, 10, 12–14, 18, 21, 28, 32, 73, 75, 79, 80, 85

encounter 4–6, 10, 21, 25–27, 34, 39, 74, 77, 80, 82, 84, 86, 87, 89, 91, 92, 100–105, 113

filiation 14, 34, 77, 83, 95

Heraclitus 8, 18, 119
holding 27, 80; inadequate 81
hypnosis 87, 92, 96, 108, 120

imprinting 83
in-between xii, 23, 24, 99, 112
Infant Care Home 20, 21, 24, 42, 46, 50, 57, 67, 69, 72
invocatory drive 77

Jullien, François 10, 12, 18, 69, 75, 79, 85, 95–97, 108, 109, 117, 119, 120

Levi, Primo 3
Lorenz, Konrad 83

maisons vertes 3
Malandrin, M.-H. 3, 12, 89
Maspero, François 3, 17, 120
maternal holding environment 27
Mauthausen 4
Modiano, Patrick 4, 9

Pictogram 80
primary narcissism 14, 94
protective shield 85

Qi 85

Rembrandt 4, 76
resonance 35, 82, 85, 103, 113
Roustang, François 86, 92, 96, 97, 108, 118, 120

Semprun, Jorge 3, 4, 17, 120

transferential effect 37
trauma 3, 4, 9, 11, 24, 29, 30, 33,
  36, 53, 55, 58, 66, 68, 70, 76,
  80, 95, 118
traumatised 12, 112

vigilance 98; generalised 96;
  heightened 86

Winnicott, Donald 10, 12, 37,
  38, 56, 74, 75, 79, 85, 120

Zhuang-Zhou 16, 86, 101, 102

For Product Safety Concerns and Information please contact our EU
representative GPSR@taylorandfrancis.com
Taylor & Francis Verlag GmbH, Kaufingerstraße 24, 80331 München, Germany

www.ingramcontent.com/pod-product-compliance
Lightning Source LLC
Chambersburg PA
CBHW050615280326
41932CB00016B/3055